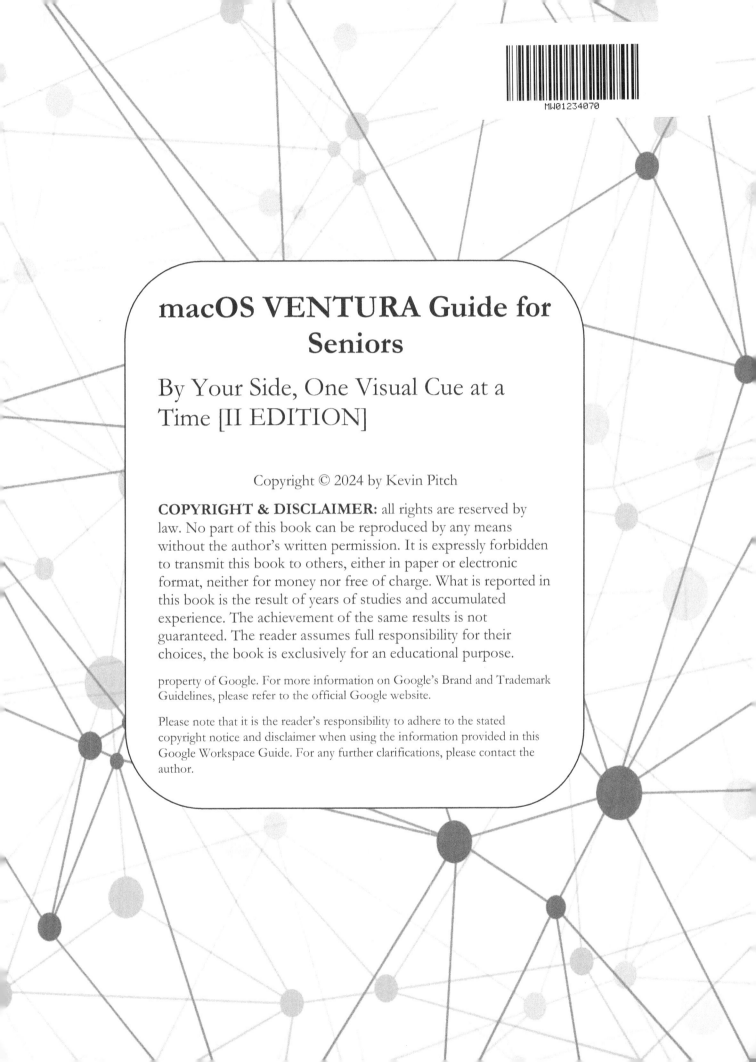

macOS VENTURA Guide for Seniors

By Your Side, One Visual Cue at a Time [II EDITION]

Copyright © 2024 by Kevin Pitch

TABLE OF CONTENTS

1   INTRODUCING MACOS VENTURA

Welcome to the dawn of a fresh digital age, where our cherished Mac undergoes a transformative rebirth. The curtain was raised at the Worldwide Developers Conference WWDC 2022, revealing the latest marvel from Apple: macOS Ventura. The announcement echoed more than just a name; it heralded a wave of innovation that would redefine the Mac experience, especially tailored for our senior audience.

Welcome to the magical world of macOS Ventura! MacOS Ventura is not just an update; it is a significant leap in the evolution of the macOS lineage. It is akin to being handed a new palette of colors after years of painting – familiar yet exhilarating. The main canvas remains, but the shades and nuances offer endless possibilities.

If you have opened this guide, there is a high chance that you are either exploring the idea of diving into the Mac universe or you have recently become a proud owner of a machine running macOS Ventura. No matter where you stand, this book serves as your doorway into a realm where technology meets simplicity, designed specifically for users like you.

You might wonder, why macOS Ventura and why now? The digital age continues to expand, and with it comes a myriad of operating systems and devices. Yet, there remains something special about the Mac, and particularly its latest iteration, macOS Ventura. It is an operating system that merges the power of innovative technology with the intuitiveness of human-centered design. And the best part? It is never too late to start.

A Fresh Start, Yet Familiar

If you have never used a Mac before, macOS Ventura will feel both fresh and inviting. Drawing inspiration from its predecessors, yet paving a new path, Ventura promises a balance of familiarity and novelty. For those migrating from other platforms, the transition is smoother than you might expect. And for complete beginners, you are in for a delightful experience where learning meets fun.

Why This Guide is for You

Senior users often get overlooked in tech manuals, which tend to assume a certain degree of tech-savviness. This guide is different. It recognizes that while you may come with a wealth of life experience and knowledge, the world of macOS might be a new frontier for you. Hence, this book is crafted with patience, care, and a genuine understanding of your needs.

Throughout these pages, we will not just talk tech; we will converse in a language that resonates with you. Expect clear, step-by-step instructions, ample visuals, and a touch of warmth and humor. We believe that technology should be accessible to all, regardless of age or previous experience, and this guide aims to bridge any gaps.

What Lies Ahead

As we embark on this journey together, you will discover the magic of the Ventura Desktop, the charm of its unique applications, and the endless possibilities it offers. From connecting with loved ones through video calls to rediscovering your favorite tunes, from setting up your device for the first time to mastering pro-tips, we have you covered. Expect the following within this guide:

- Understanding what macOS Ventura is and the key features
- Basic terminology used
- Functioning of Ventura's Desktop and Finder
- Basic tasks like turning on, guided instruction on the screen, quick start, manual configuration, open and save files, file, and folder management
- Apps born in iOS
- Essentials apps to chat and email.
- Videocalls.
- Create a document
- Manage the music
- How to share contents
- How to do the backup and use iCloud
- Getting to know about widgets
- How to connect the iPhone to your laptop
- Most common and life saver tips and tricks
- FAQs

So, whether you are looking to reignite an old passion, embark on a new hobby, or simply navigate the digital age with ease and confidence, macOS Ventura is your trusty companion, and this guide is your roadmap.

2 What's macOS Ventura

Imagine taking a journey through a vast digital landscape, one where your every step is anticipated, your needs are met with intuitive solutions, and you are constantly surrounded by sleek, elegant design. This is the experience of macOS Ventura, Apple's newest operating system for their line of Mac computers. But let us strip away the technical jargon and address the core question: What is macOS Ventura?

A Fresh Face in the Mac Family

macOS Ventura is the latest in an extensive line of Apple operating systems. If you think of these operating systems as generations in a family, then macOS Ventura is the newest member, benefiting from the wisdom of its predecessors while bringing its own innovations to the table.

The Heart of Your Computer

Every computer requires an operating system (or OS). It is the software that powers the machine, allowing all its components to work in harmony. It lets you type, browse the web, listen to music, and so much more. macOS Ventura is the very heart and brain of your Mac computer, offering a user-friendly interface, a vast array of features, and the promise of stability and security.

Blend of Simplicity and Power

What sets macOS Ventura apart is its perfect balance of simplicity and power. It is designed to be approachable, especially for those who might not consider themselves 'tech-savvy.' At the same time, underneath its sleek surface lies a robust and advanced operating system, capable of performing complex tasks with ease.

Seamless Integration with Other Apple Devices

One of the standout features of macOS Ventura is its ability to work seamlessly with other Apple devices. If you own an iPhone, iPad, or even an Apple Watch, you will find that these devices can communicate with your Mac in ways that feel almost magical. Share photos, answer calls, or even copy text from one device and paste it onto another - macOS Ventura makes it all possible.

A Focus on Privacy and Security

In today's digital age, privacy and security are paramount. macOS Ventura is built with this in mind, incorporating state-of-the-art security features to protect your data and ensure your online safety. From safeguarding your personal photos to preventing malicious software attacks, you can trust that macOS Ventura is looking out for you.

Endless Opportunities with Apps

At its core, macOS Ventura provides a platform for thousands of applications (or apps). These apps, ranging from productivity tools to entertainment suites, allow you to customize your Mac experience to fit your unique needs and passions.

At the heart of Ventura is the **Stage Manager**, a multitasking marvel that ensures you always have what you need, precisely when you need it. Picture this: Your primary app stands proudly at the forefront, while others, like trusty aides, wait in the wings, ready to be summoned. And the beauty is in the fluidity – whether you are transitioning between tasks or adjusting your workflow, Stage Manager, coupled with Mission Control and Spaces, ensures seamless navigation.

Have you ever lamented the quality of your Mac's camera? With the introduction of **Continuity Camera**, those days are behind us. Your iPhone is not just a phone anymore; it is a potential high-quality webcam for your Mac. Whether showcasing your workspace with the Ultra-Wide lens or using the Studio Light effect to shine the spotlight on you during a call, your iPhone's camera steps up to elevate the video experience.

Communication receives a transformative touch in Ventura. **Handoff** now embraces FaceTime, bridging the gap between your Mac and iPhone. Meanwhile, **Messages** not only let you undo those occasional typos or retract hastily sent texts but also introduces collaboration at a level previously uncharted. Sharing, discussing, and editing documents becomes a social activity, integrating work and chat seamlessly.

Ventura's **Mail app** is reborn. It is smarter, faster, and more intuitive. Whether you are searching for an old email or scheduling a future one, Mail ensures a user-friendly experience. Ever felt that pang of regret after hitting 'send'? Now, you have a 10-second window to undo. And with intelligent features like automatic follow-up suggestions and context-based detections, Mail is no longer just a communication tool; it is an assistant.

MacOS Ventura welcomes new members to its app family. The **Weather** and **Clock apps**, familiar faces from iOS, make their Mac debut. And for those accustomed to System Preferences, prepare for a refreshing change with the newly named **System Settings**, echoing its iPhone and iPad counterparts in design and function.

With every iteration of macOS, Apple endeavors to simplify our digital lives, and with Ventura, they have certainly not held back.

Collaborative Browsing in Safari

The Safari experience is no longer a solitary one. With the **Shared Tab Groups** feature, browsing is transformed into a collaborative endeavor. Whether you are assembling a list of websites for a family project or creating bookmarks for a vacation, sharing and collaborating is just a click away. Moreover, initiating a **Messages conversation or FaceTime call directly from Safari** brings a seamless integration between browsing and communication - perfect for live discussions on project research or a surprise vacation spot.

A New Dawn for Digital Security

Gone are the days of juggling countless passwords and worrying about their security. Enter **Passkeys** – the vanguard of digital credentials. Designed to be stored only on your device and away from vulnerable web servers, Passkeys offers an unparalleled level of security. The cherry on top? Ease of use. With **Touch ID or Face ID authentication** and the flexibility of syncing across devices through iCloud Keychain, this feature is not just a security upgrade, but also a user experience revolution.

Spotlight Shines Brighter

Ventura's **Spotlight** is not just a search tool; it is a dynamic assistant. Its refined design, coupled with **Quick Look** offers instantaneous previews of files. Dive into your memories effortlessly as the Photo Library integration allows searches by location, people, scenes, and even objects. Ever thought of extracting text from an image? **Live Text** makes it a reality. Furthermore, Spotlight enriches your search results, giving detailed insights into artists, movies, businesses, and more.

Unlocking the Power of Visual Look Up

Ventura brings the magic of **Visual Look Up**, a feature that feels right out of a sci-fi novel. Ever wondered about a bird you captured in a photo or intrigued by a statue? Now, not only can you recognize these entities, but you can also effortlessly drag and drop them into different apps. It is digital interaction on a whole new level.

Bonding Over Shared Memories

The **iCloud Shared Photo Library** is a nod to family moments and shared memories. With the capacity to include up to six family members, this library acts as a shared canvas where every member can contribute, edit, or even highlight their favorite snaps. Plus, intelligent sharing suggestions means you are always reminded of those cherished moments.

A Gaming Metamorphosis

Gamers, rejoice! macOS Ventura introduces **Metal 3**, tailored to uplift the gaming experience on Apple silicon Macs. With **MetalFX Upscaling** and the **Fast Resource Loading API**, games are not only visually captivating but also remarkably responsive. Every frame, texture, and in-game element are rendered with unprecedented fidelity.

Enhanced Security Protocols

Security remains paramount with macOS Ventura. The introduction of the **Rapid Security Response** feature underscores this commitment. Now, security updates can be seamlessly installed without the need for a complete system overhaul or even a reboot. It is a testament to how macOS Ventura prioritizes user convenience without compromising on security.

2.1 The Main Features of macOS Ventura

Diving into macOS Ventura is akin to unwrapping a present – with each layer you uncover, there is another delightful surprise waiting for you. This section will introduce you to the standout features of macOS Ventura, tailored especially for our senior readers who might be navigating this digital landscape for the first time.

1. User-Friendly Interface

Ventura's Clean Aesthetics: With a crisp, modern design, macOS Ventura presents an interface that is a pleasure to the eyes. Icons are clear, fonts are legible, and everything is organized for intuitive access.

2. Enhanced Accessibility Features

VoiceOver Improvements: This feature reads out the content on the screen, and with Ventura, it is smoother and more accurate than ever.

Magnifier and Larger Text Options: For those with visual impairments, macOS Ventura offers the ability to magnify portions of the screen or increase text size for easier reading.

3. Handoff and Continuity

Easily transition between your Mac, iPhone, and iPad. Start an email on your iPhone and finish it on your Mac or copy a photo on your Mac and paste it into a document on your iPad, all without missing a beat.

4. Siri Integration

Just like on the iPhone and iPad, Siri – Apple's voice-activated assistant – is now more integrated into Ventura. Ask Siri to find files, play music, answer queries, and more, all with a simple voice command.

5. Improved Messaging Capabilities

Ventura allows users to pin important conversations, mention specific people, and even integrates more expressive message effects, making digital communication livelier and more personal.

6. Focus Mode

This feature lets you customize notifications based on what you are doing, ensuring that distractions are minimized. Whether you are watching a movie, attending a virtual meeting, or reading, Focus Mode ensures your digital environment is conducive to the task at hand.

7. Redesigned Safari Browser

Browsing the web is a key part of the modern computer experience. Ventura's Safari comes with a redesigned interface, grouped tabs, and enhanced privacy features, ensuring a safe and smooth surfing experience.

8. Universal Control

For those with multiple Apple devices, Universal Control is a meaningful change. It allows you to use a single mouse and keyboard to navigate between your Mac, iPad, and even iPhone.

9. Revamped Maps Application

Discover new places or revisit old memories with the enhanced Maps app. It offers detailed city experiences, an interactive globe view, and even more detailed driving directions.

10. Quick Note Feature

Need to jot down a quick thought or reminder? With Quick Note, you can swiftly create notes from any application or website, making sure you never miss capturing valuable information.

11. Enhanced Privacy Features

macOS Ventura places a strong emphasis on protecting user data. With features like Mail Privacy Protection and an updated Mac App Store highlighting privacy practice of apps, you can be assured of a secure digital environment.

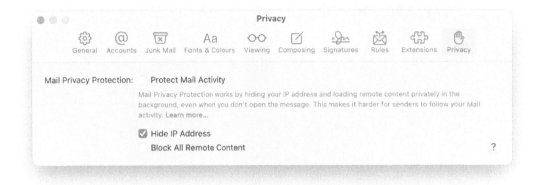

12. Dynamic Desktop and New Wallpapers

Ventura introduces dynamic desktops that change based on the time of day, reflecting morning, afternoon, and night. This, paired with a collection of stunning new wallpapers, ensures a visually refreshing experience each time you use your Mac.

Navigating the latest macOS can be overwhelming, especially for seniors who might be used to older versions. macOS Ventura comes with a suite of features designed to make Mac usage more intuitive, efficient, and enjoyable Here is a simplified guide tailored for seniors, unpacking the essential features of macOS Ventura:

1. Stage Manager: Simplifying Your Screen

- **Distraction-Free**: The feature organizes your active windows, pushing them to the side and highlighting the application you are using.

- **Easy App Grouping**: Simply drag and drop apps on top of each other to form a group. Handy thumbnails make it easy to switch between these groupings.

- **Collaborate with iPad**: Move applications seamlessly between your Mac and an iPad, making multitasking smoother.

2. Spotlight: Your Search Genius

- **Quick Look**: Preview individual search results just by tapping the spacebar.

- **Enhanced Search**: Apart from browsing your Photo Library, Spotlight can now delve deep into individual images, run shortcuts, and much more.

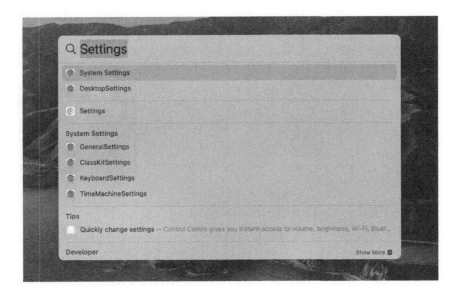

3. Mail: More Than Just Email

- **Recall Sent Emails**: Made an error in your email? Now, you can take it back.

- **Scheduled Sends**: Plan by scheduling when your emails get sent.

- **Search Made Simple**: As you start typing, Mail will suggest search terms, helping you locate shared documents, links, and attachments with greater accuracy.

4. Safari: A Browser that Understands Teamwork

- **Shared Tab Groups**: Collaboratively create and share lists of tabs and links with friends or colleagues.

- **PassKey**: A leap in security, this new feature does away with the need for traditional passwords, offering a more secure sign-in method that cannot be easily compromised.

5. FaceTime Continuity: Smooth Transitions

Switch from a FaceTime call on your iPhone to your Mac effortlessly. Your Mac shows a simple switch button for a seamless transfer.

6. Continuity Camera: Enhancing Virtual Presence

- **Your iPhone as a Webcam**: With wireless technology, your iPhone can now function as a dynamic webcam for your Mac.

- **Deskview**: Highlight your desk items during virtual meetings. Compatible with popular platforms like Zoom, Teams, and Webex.

- **Improved Imaging**: Features like Portrait Mode and Studio Light make you look your best during calls.

7. System Settings: Familiar Yet New

- **Redesigned for Intuitiveness**: The renamed 'System Settings' menu mirrors the layout on iOS devices, making it more recognizable for those familiar with Apple's mobile interfaces.

- **Easier Wi-Fi Access**: No more digging deep into network settings. Wi-Fi gets its dedicated spot, emphasizing its importance in everyday use.

- **Suggestions at the Forefront**: While the exact function remains secret, it is speculated to give tailored recommendations for optimizing your device settings.

2.2 Devices that Support MacOS Ventura

Navigating the technicalities of device compatibility can be a daunting task for seniors, especially when transitioning to the latest macOS. With the introduction of macOS Ventura, Apple continues its tradition of supporting a broad range of devices. However, understanding which ones are compatible is crucial to ensure a seamless experience. Below is a tailored guide to help seniors understand which devices are poised to run macOS Ventura:

A Quick Insight into Apple's Chip Evolution

Apple's transition to its in-house M1 and M2 silicon chips represents a significant leap in performance and energy conservation. However, this advanced technology brings about questions on longevity and compatibility, especially for older devices.

While these powerful chips might imply a shift towards exclusive support for the latest devices, Apple maintains a commitment to backward compatibility. This commitment ensures that even some older Macs, especially those powered by Intel, are not left behind.

Is Your Mac Ready for macOS Ventura?

Ventura, the 13th iteration of the macOS, extends its support to a varied range of Mac devices, both old and new. Here is a simplified list for a quick check:

1. **iMac**: All models from 2017 and later. This includes the specialized 2017 iMac Pro, tailored for professional users.

2. **MacBook**: Every model from 2017 onwards. A great fit for those who prioritize portability without compromising on performance.

3. **MacBook Pro**: Devices released from 2017 and after. Designed for power users who require a bit more oomph in their daily tasks.

4. **MacBook Air**: Models starting from 2018 and later. A blend of performance and lightweight design for everyday users.

5. **Mac mini**: All variations from 2018 and beyond. A compact powerhouse suitable for various tasks.

6. **Mac Pro**: Starting from 2019 models. The epitome of computing prowess, tailored for professionals with demanding needs.

7. **Mac Studio**: Introduced in 2022, this is the newest addition to the family, promising unmatched performance.

3   Basic terminology

Navigating a new operating system can be a daunting task, especially with the bevy of terms and jargon that come with it. For our senior readers who are either new to macOS Ventura or looking for a refresher, this guide breaks down the basic terminology to help make your experience smooth and enjoyable.

1. Desktop

When you start up your Mac, the very first screen you see is the Desktop. Think of it as your virtual workspace, a place where your files, folders, and apps live and can be accessed. The background image, or 'wallpaper', can be customized to your liking.

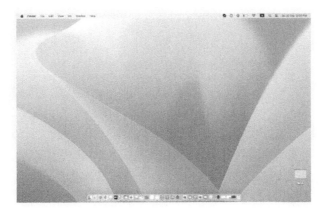

2. Dock

At the bottom of your screen, you will notice a bar with icons – this is the Dock. It is a quick-access hub (or shortcuts) for your favorite applications, files, documents, and folders. Clicking an icon launches the app, and if the app is already open, it helps you switch to it.

3. Finder

If macOS was a house, Finder would be your guide. It is the app you use to dig through and organize your files and applications, like browsing through files in a filing cabinet.

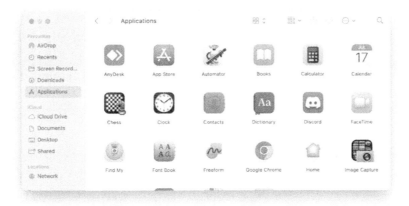

4. Menu Bar

Look at the top of your screen, and you will see a horizontal bar. This is the Menu Bar. It offers a variety of system functions, like checking the Wi-Fi, adjusting volume, or accessing app-specific options.

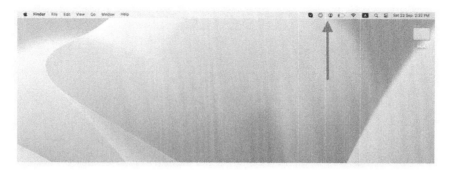

5. Spotlight

Cannot find a file, data or an app? Enter Spotlight. By pressing Command + Space, you can activate Spotlight and instantly search for anything on your Mac.

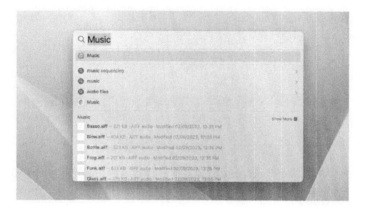

6. System Preferences

Think of System Preferences as your control room. It is where you can adjust settings, tweak your display, change security options, and more. It is like the Control Panel on Windows.

7. iCloud

Apple's cloud storage and syncing service. iCloud is like a virtual locker, safekeeping your photos, documents, and other data. It also ensures that your data is consistent across all your Apple devices.

8. Mission Control

Overwhelmed by too many open windows? Enter Mission Control. With a swipe or a click, you get an aerial view of all open windows and virtual desktops, making it easier to switch between tasks.

9. Stage Manager

New to macOS Ventura, Stage Manager is your stage director, ensuring you focus on one act (or app) at a time by clearing distractions and bringing your current task front and center.

10. Shared Tab Groups

In Safari, macOS Ventura's web browser, Shared Tab Groups is your research assistant. It lets you create a bundle of related tabs and share them with friends or colleagues.

11. PassKey

Gone are the days of juggling countless passwords. With PassKey in Safari, your online identity gets a high-security easy-to-use upgrade. It is a unique digital key that verifies your identity without traditional passwords.

12. FaceTime Continuity

A feature that allows users to hand off an active FaceTime call from an iPhone to a Mac. Ever started a FaceTime call on your iPhone and wished to continue your Mac's larger screen? With FaceTime Continuity, making the switch is seamless.

13. Continuity Camera

Your iPhone's camera can now be your Mac's webcam. This feature is especially handy for video calls, giving a clearer, more versatile camera experience.

14. Deskview

During video calls, Deskview acts like a second set of eyes, focusing on items on your desk, such as documents or drawings. It is like having an overhead projector for your virtual meetings.

15. System Settings

Previously known as "System Preferences," System Settings is your Mac's command center with a fresh look. If you have used an iPad or iPhone, the layout will feel familiar.

Mac App Store: A digital distribution platform for macOS apps.

Time Machine: The built-in backup feature of macOS.

Siri: Apple's voice-controlled personal assistant.

AirDrop: A feature that allows quick and easy file transfers between Apple devices.

Touch ID/Face ID: Biometric authentication methods for verifying identity on compatible Mac models.

Wallpapers

Every computer has a backdrop image when you are looking at your Desktop. In macOS, these backdrop images are referred to as Wallpapers. macOS Ventura offers a collection of pre-loaded images, but you can also set personal photos as your wallpaper for a more customized touch.

Status Menus

On the right-hand side of the Menu Bar at the top of your screen, you will see a set of icons. These icons, known as Status Menus, provide a quick look and access to system settings and features like Wi-Fi, battery status, volume, and more.

Launchpad

Imagine having all your apps displayed in a neat grid. That is Launchpad for you. Accessible through an icon in the Dock or a pinch gesture on a trackpad, Launchpad showcases all your applications in an iPad-like view, allowing you to quickly launch any app.

Trash

When you delete a file or application, it goes to the Trash. Think of it as a digital waste bin. Files in the trash are not yet permanently deleted; they are merely set aside. To permanently delete them, you need to "empty" the trash. But remember, once emptied, those files are gone for good.

Activity Monitor

Ever wondered what is happening behind the scenes on your Mac? Activity Monitor is your backstage pass. This utility provides a detailed look at system processes, memory usage, and application activity. If an application is not responding, the Activity Monitor lets you force quit it.

Aliases

An alias in macOS is a shortcut to a file or application, letting you access it quickly from a location of your choice, like the Desktop. It is like having a duplicate of your file without taking up extra storage.

Keychain

Think of Keychain as a digital vault. It securely stores your passwords, making it easier to manage and auto-fill login information for various websites and apps.

Spaces

Spaces are virtual desktops in macOS, allowing you to organize your windows and applications into separate groups. This is especially handy when multitasking or working on different projects.

Force Touch

On certain Mac trackpads, pressing harder, or "force touching," can activate additional options or features. For instance, force touching a word might bring up its definition.

Time Machine

This is macOS's built-in backup system. With Time Machine, your Mac takes periodic snapshots of your files and allows you to go "back in time" to recover older versions or accidentally deleted files.

4   Installing macOS Ventura

Navigating the complex world of software installations can be daunting, especially with beta versions which may be a tad more complicated than the usual updates. Fear not! Here is a step-by-step guide to help you download and install macOS 13 Ventura with ease.

1. Understand What You're Getting Into

- macOS Ventura is still in its public beta phase. This means that while everyone can try it, it is not the definitive version. This also means potential glitches and issues. Apple suggests not installing it on your main Mac. If you have an older or secondary Mac, use that for this test run.

2. Backup, Backup, Backup!

- Safety first! Always back up your data before making any significant changes to your system.

- Use Apple's Time Machine feature to save everything onto an external drive.

- This backup will be your safety net if you decide to revert to your older macOS or face any challenges.

3. Enrolling in the Apple Beta Software Program

- Before you can download Ventura, you need to sign up for Apple's Beta Software Program.

- Go to the Apple Beta Software Program website.

- Click on the blue "Sign up" or "Sign in" if you are already a member.

- Follow the steps to sign in using your Apple ID.

- Agree to the terms and conditions.

- Now, at the top of the page, click on "Enroll Your Devices." Then, select "macOS."

4. Downloading the macOS Ventura Beta

- Once you have enrolled, navigate to the macOS section.

- Scroll down to "Enroll your Mac" and click "Download the macOS Public Beta Access Utility."

- If prompted, click "Allow" to approve downloads from "beta.apple.com."

- Find the downloaded file (macOSPublicBetaAccessUtility.dmg) in your downloads folder and double-click on it.

- Double-click the **.pkg** file within and follow the instructions.

- When the download is completed, the installer will launch the System Preferences Software Update panel. Here, you will see the macOS 13 Beta download.

5. Installing macOS Ventura

- Click "Upgrade Now" to start downloading the beta software.

- Once downloaded, your Mac will restart.

- After rebooting, if the macOS 13 installer does not start automatically, find it in your "applications" folder.

- Click "Continue" and follow the on-screen steps.

- Agree to terms and conditions and confirm you have created a backup.

- Choose the disk where you want to install the beta (either your computer's main drive or a created partition).

- Click "Install," provide your administrator password, and restart your Mac.

- After restarting, the installation of macOS 13 begins. Once it finishes and your Mac reboots, you will be running the macOS Ventura public beta!

Remember, installing beta software is like a sneak peek into what is to come. While it is exciting, it is also prone to unexpected issues. So, always ensure you are comfortable with the process and keep your data safe. Enjoy exploring macOS Ventura!

5   Customizing the Dock

You have a lot of control over the Dock's settings, so you can customize it to seem more like your own. If you want to modify either its size or its position, you can do so using the System Settings in the following manner:

The steps:

1. In the upper-left-hand corner of your display, click the **Apple menu** to open it on your Mac.

2. Navigate to the **System Settings option**.

3. Choose **Desktop & Dock** from the menu.

Resize the Dock

A slider that lets you modify the amount of space used by your program Dock can be found right at the very top. Modify it so that it fits your tastes perfectly.

You will notice an option to Position on the screen just below the slider that controls the size. Simply tap it to choose between the Left, the Bottom, and the Right option.

Voila! Now the application Dock on your Mac will be the size you want it to be and will be placed where you want it.

Add a Spacer to the Dock

When it comes to personalizing the Dock, the option to add spacers is one of the best-hidden features that can be found.

You cannot create standard folders for the various kinds of programs, this makes it much simpler to arrange apps according to their categories or just to group them.

The steps:

1. Launch the **Terminal application** on your Mac.

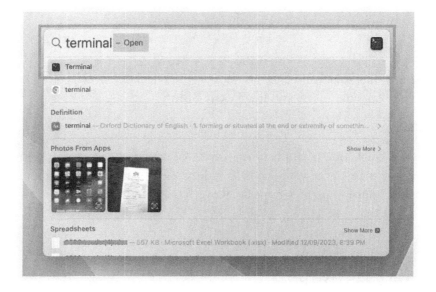

2. Type the following command:

- defaults write com. apple. dock persistent-apps-

- array-add '{"tile-type"="spacer-tile";}'; killall Dock

3. Select **Enter**.

When you hit the Enter key, the Dock will momentarily vanish, and any applications that were previously minimized will become visible on the screen. After the procedure is finished, there will be a void at the very end of your dock to which you may move your items.

After that, you can move the spacer about any way you see fit, positioning it in between other applications to create a cluster of them all at once.

Hide Recent Applications

After completing the preliminary steps of the setup procedure, the first thing that you should do is to **"declutter"** the Dock by removing any unnecessary items.

The steps:

1. Launch **System Settings**.

2. Click **Desktop and Dock**.

3. Select the **"Show recent apps in Dock"** option and click the **"Check"** button.

The additional part on the Dock will vanish as soon as the checkbox is selected, leaving you with just the programs that you want, the Downloads folder, and the **Trash Bin**.

Adjust Magnification

When it comes to the Dock, one useful feature is that you can choose to have the programs enlarged anytime your mouse is lingering over them. You will be able to reduce the size of the dock by doing so, but you will still be able to click and access the appropriate programs whenever you want them.

The steps:

1. Launch **System Settings**.

2. Click **Desktop & Dock**.

3. Select the **"Magnification" checkbox** and click **the "Check" button**.

4. Make the necessary adjustments to the slider.

When you are making use of the Magnification feature on the Dock, you will want to make certain that the slider is moved to a position that is higher than that of the **"Size" option**. This makes it so that the icons in the Dock will get larger when the cursor is moved over them in that area.

Add and Remove Apps from the Dock

When it comes to personalizing the Dock, one of the fundamental features is the ability to add or remove applications. When you do this, it guarantees that the only applications that display are the ones that you use the most often even when all your other apps are closed.

The steps:

1. Open **Launchpad** by clicking its icon in the Dock.

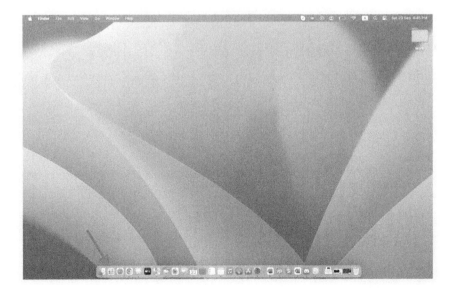

2. Find the application that you want to add to the Dock and click its icon.

3. Move the app to the position on the Dock that you want it to be in by dragging and dropping it there.

Right-click on the application you want to keep in the Dock, choose **Options** from the drop-down menu, and then select the **Keep in Dock option**.

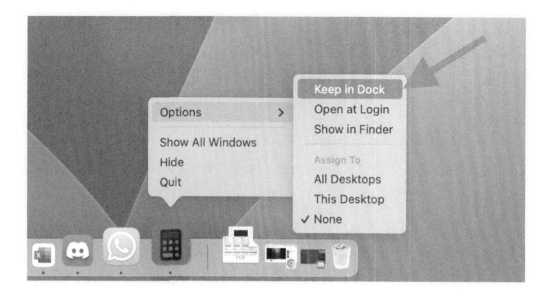

If you want the Dock to seem more personal to you, you will want to get rid of any applications that you do not plan to use in the future. This is the procedure for removing applications from the Dock.

The steps:

1. Using Spotlight, search for the application that you wish to delete from the Dock.

2. Right-click the app.

3. Using your pointer, highlight the Options menu.

4. Select the **"Remove from Dock"** option.

If the application that you want to remove from the Dock is already open, you can delete it by clicking and holding it, dragging it away from the Dock, and then releasing it.

Add Folders to the Dock

The Downloads and Trash Can folders be already there in the Dock. However, it is also possible to add more folders to the dock.

The steps:

1. On your Mac, launch the **Finder application**.

2. Go to the folder that you want to add to the Dock, and then click the **Add button**.

3. Select **Open Folder** from the context menu.

4. Select **"Add to Dock"** from the submenu of the drop-down menu.

6   Functioning of Ventura's Desktop and Finder

Here is the heart of your Mac - the desktop and Finder in macOS Ventura. Imagine stepping into a well-organized office: every file in its place, every tool within reach, and a helpful assistant (let us call him 'Finder') always ready to help. That is precisely what Ventura's Desktop and Finder aim to replicate for you, digitally.

6.1   Ventura's Lively Desktop

Think of your desktop as the top of a real desk. In the physical world, you might have photos, papers, or pens scattered about. On your Mac:

- **Wallpaper**: Set the mood! Your desktop background can be a beautiful preset image or a cherished personal photo. With Ventura, every time you open your laptop, it is like glancing at a favorite view or a loved one's picture.

- **Status Menus**: At the top right, you will find tiny icons showing battery life, Wi-Fi strength, and the time. It is like the little clocks, calendars, and indicators we keep on our real desks to stay informed.

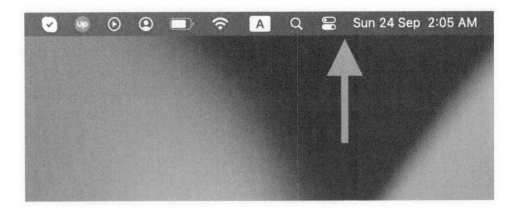

- **Sticky Notes**: Want to jot down a quick reminder? With macOS Ventura, you can stick digital notes right on your desktop.

Ventura's desktop is not just a screen; it is a canvas of possibilities. For many seniors, this digital realm might feel like a foreign land, but fear not! Like learning to read a new book or paint a picture, understanding this canvas can be a delightful journey. Here is your map.

Step 1: Setting Foot on Ventura's Vibrant Landscape

As soon as you boot up your Mac, you are greeted by the desktop - a serene backdrop, often a scenic view, which you can personalize. This is your digital 'home.'

- **Wallpapers**: Feel free to customize your desktop background. Click on the Apple menu > System Preferences > Desktop & Screen Saver. From here, select a wallpaper that resonates with your spirit - a nostalgic photograph or a calming nature scene.

Step 2: The Desktop Icons - Your Handy Tools and Files

Sprinkled on this canvas are icons: tiny pictures representing your files, folders, and connected drives.

- **Files & Folders**: Think of these as digital versions of paper documents and folders. Click to open and drag to move.

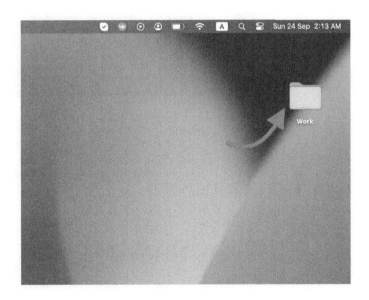

- **Hard Drives & Devices**: When you connect a USB stick or an external hard drive, its icon appears on the desktop. Like plugging in a lamp into a socket and seeing it light up.

Step 3: The Dock - Your Digital Toolbelt

At the bottom (or side) is your Dock, a bar of icons. Think of it as a handy toolbelt, where your most-used applications rest.

- **Applications**: From Mail to Safari, click on these icons to launch the apps.

- **Folders**: Some special folders, like Downloads or Documents, might also be on the Dock for easy access.

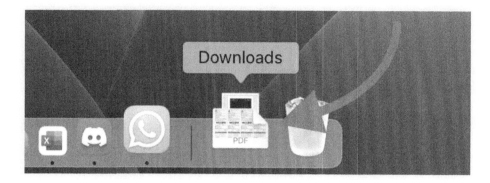

- **Trash**: On the far right, there is the Trash can. Drag unwanted files here to discard or click to see what is inside before emptying.

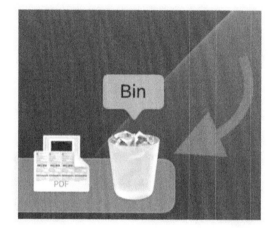

Step 4: The Menu Bar - A Compass for Your Journey

Running along the top is the Menu Bar, holding various menus and icons.

- **Apple Menu**: Click the Apple logo on the top-left to access fundamental controls. Here you can sleep, restart, or shut down your Mac, and dive into System Preferences.

- **Application Menus**: This change depending on the application you are using. When in Safari, you will see options related to web browsing. In Mail, you will find email-related actions.

- **Status Menus**: On the right side of the Menu Bar are tiny indicators. These show Wi-Fi strength, battery status, date, and time - like little signposts keeping you informed on your journey.

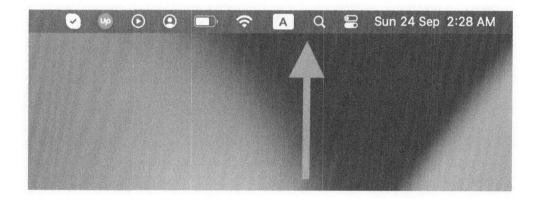

Step 5: Right-Click – The Magic Wand

On your desktop, a 'right-click' (or two-finger tap on the trackpad) reveals hidden menus. It is like a magic wand, revealing shortcuts and actions related to whatever you click on. Use it on a file, folder, or even the desktop's empty space to unveil its secrets.

6.2 Meet 'Finder': Your Digital Assistant

Remember our friendly assistant from the office analogy? In the digital realm, which is the Finder. It helps you navigate your Mac's files and folders:

- **The Friendly Blue Face**: Finder is always ready to help! Click on its smiley blue face, usually resting in your Dock, and you are off to explore your Mac.

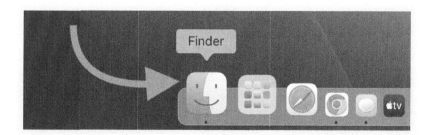

- **Navigating With Ease**: Once opened, Finder presents your files and folders in a neat window. On the left sidebar, you will find shortcuts to your favorite locations like "Documents" or "Downloads."

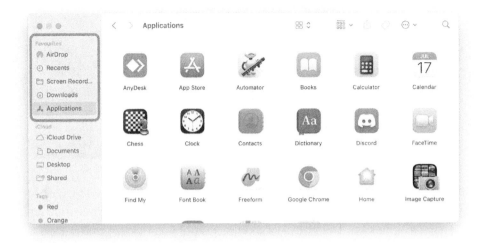

- **Search in Snap**: Can't find a file? No problem! At the top right of any Finder window is a search bar. Just type in what you are looking for, and the Finder will fetch it.

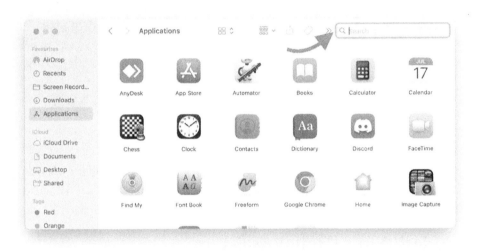

- **Quick Look**: Highlight a file and press the space bar. A quick preview pops up, letting you peek inside without fully opening it. It is like glancing at the contents of an envelope without removing everything.

- **Tabs & Tags**: Remember those color-coded sticky tabs we use in physical folders? Finder lets you tag you files with colorful labels, making them easy to spot. And just like in a web browser, you can open multiple tabs in Finder to jump between folders swiftly.

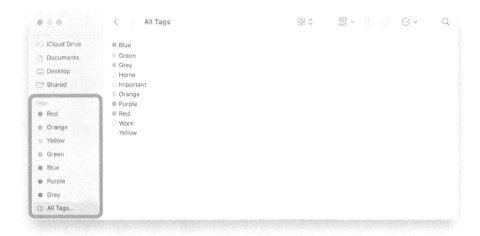

Step 1: Spotting the Lighthouse – The Finder Icon

Begin at the Dock, where amidst various icons, you will spot a smiling, two-toned blue face. That is our lighthouse, our beacon: the Finder. A single click, and you are aboard your ship, ready to sail!

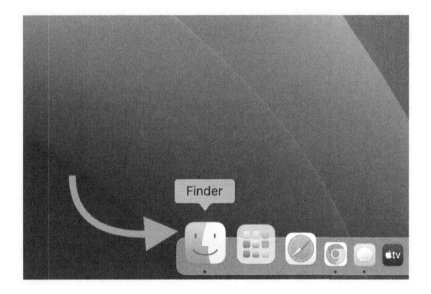

Step 2: Navigating the Oceans – The Finder Window

Once inside, the Finder window appears like a vast ocean, teeming with life.

- **Sidebar**: On the left, there is a vertical list. These are your favorite ports, the frequently visited islands: Documents, Downloads, Applications, and more. A single click transports you right to that island!

- **Main Area**: This displays the content of whichever location (or 'island') you have selected, be it files, folders, or other mysterious treasures.

Step 3: Setting Your Sails – The Toolbar

At the window's top, a bar of icons and options—the Toolbar—acts as your sails and compass combined.

- **Back & Forward Arrows**: These let you retrace your steps, or move forward, just like navigating the high seas.

- **View Buttons**: Spot the four tiny icons? They change how your treasures (files and folders) are displayed. Icons, list, columns, or a gallery view - choose as per your whimsy!

- **Search**: A magnifying glass sits ready. Type in, and it will search the vast oceans to find your lost treasures.

Step 4: The Magical Maps – Finder Tabs and Windows

- **Multiple Windows**: If one ship is not enough, open another! Simply choose File > New Finder Window. Now, you can sail to different islands simultaneously.

- **Tabs**: Prefer keeping all maps in one place? Finder tabs are akin to multiple maps in one book. Click File > New Tab, and a new tab appears, letting you explore multiple islands within one window.

Step 5: The Hidden Coves – Right-Click Secrets

Like any good treasure map, there are secrets in Finder. 'Right-click' (or a two-finger tap on trackpads) on any file or folder. Lo and behold! A menu of actions appears, unveiling shortcuts, hidden pathways, and secret coves.

Step 6: Tagging Your Treasures

In Finder, you can 'tag' your files and folders with colorful labels. Think of them as magical seals, denoting importance, category, or just for fun. A right-click, and choosing a color, adorns your treasure with its seal.

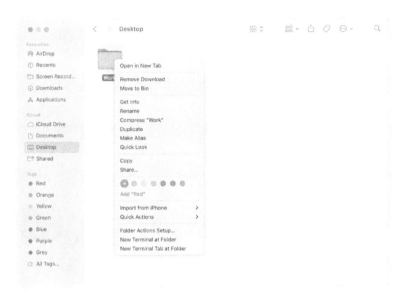

Step 7: Sharing Your Bounty

Found something worth sharing? The share button (a box with an upward arrow) in the Finder window lets you share your digital treasures. Send via Mail, AirDrop, or Messages. Spread the joy of discovery!

6.3 Customizing Your Command Center

Ventura's Desktop and Finder are adaptable. Do you prefer larger icons? Or a different view of your files? With a few clicks:

- **Icon Sizing**: Use the slider at the bottom right of any Finder window to adjust icon sizes.

- **View Options**: At the top of the Finder window, you will find four tiny buttons. These allow you to switch between icon, list, column, and gallery views. Try them out and choose what feels best!

- **Sorting Magic**: Right-click (or two-finger tap on a trackpad) in any open space within Finder. You will see options to "Sort By." Whether it is by name, date, or size, Finder will organize it mfor you.

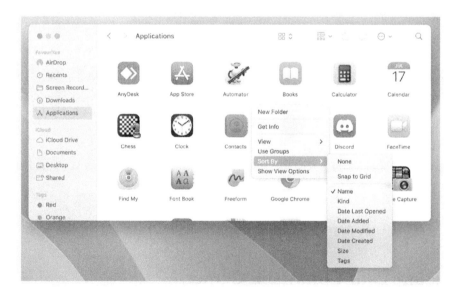

7 Basic tasks: Set-up Procedure

Your journey into the expansive sea of macOS Ventura begins with charting the setup procedure.

Pressing the Power Button

Your journey starts with a simple gesture, reminiscent of drawing back the curtains to let the light in.

- **Locate the Button**: On the MacBook, the power button, subtly marked with a touch of a square or in some, an old-world 'Touch ID', usually rests in the upper-right corner of the keyboard. For iMacs, the round button awaits behind the left edge of the screen, like a secret sunrise.

- **A Gentle Caress**: Gently press the button. It is like coaxing the sun to rise. A soft touch is all it takes.

A Symphony of Sound: The Chime

As birds herald the new day, so does the Mac with its iconic chime. It is macOS Ventura's way of whispering, "Welcome back, explorer."

The Horizon Emerges: The Apple Logo

Just as the sun's arc takes form on the horizon, the Apple logo shall grace your screen—a beacon guiding you to vast digital landscapes.

The Welcome Screen

Once your macOS Ventura awakens, a welcoming embrace in the form of an initial setup screen will appear. This is not just an interface—it is like a friendly lighthouse keeper waving you in.

- **Choose Your Language**: With an array of languages displayed, select the one that feels most like home. It is Ventura's way of asking, "In which language shall we converse, dear traveler?"

Morning's Warm Embrace: The Login Screen

As the morning fog unveils landscapes, macOS Ventura reveals its login screen, your gateway to the day's adventures.

- **Your Name and Visage**: If you have personalized your Mac, you will spot your name and a chosen picture. It is macOS Ventura's way of saying, "I recognize you, dear traveler."

- **Entering the Realm**: Click or tap on your name or image. A field emerges, beckoning you to key in your password—the secret passphrase to your digital kingdom.

Daybreak's Full Splendor: The Desktop

Having entered the passphrase, like the sun in all its mid-morning glory, the Ventura desktop unveils itself. Icons shimmer like dew-kissed leaves and the dock rests at the screen's base, like a quiet stream awaiting exploration.

And we go to the main set up.

1. The First Glimpse: Welcome to Ventura's Horizon

Your Mac, upon its maiden power-up, will greet you with a sunlit horizon – the *Welcome Screen*.

- **Port of Call**: You'll be asked to pick your native shores (your country or region). This helps Ventura tailor your experience to local settings and nuances.

2. The Navigator's Tool: Choosing Your Keyboard

Every explorer needs a reliable compass. Your Mac's compass is its keyboard.

- **Select a Layout**: From the familiar QWERTY to others like AZERTY, pick what feels right. You are the captain here; steer in a way that feels home!

3. Catching the Wind: Connecting to Wi-Fi

To sail the vast digital ocean, you will need the winds of the internet.

- **Spot Wi-Fi Signal**: Your Mac will search for nearby Wi-Fi signals like a sailor looking for land.
- **Docking**: Click on your preferred network, enter the password, and drop your digital anchor!

4. The Explorer's Chronicle: Setting Up Apple ID

The legends of your digital journey are penned down with the Apple ID – your key to Apple's treasure trove.

- **Existing ID**: If you've previously sailed Apple's waters, enter your Apple ID and password.
- **New Voyage**: New to the seas? Click "Create Apple ID" and follow the map.
- **Solo Sailing**: Prefer a quiet sail without an ID? Click "Set Up Later."

5. Agreeing to the Sea Code: Terms and Conditions

Every sea has its code. Apple's is in the form of *Terms & Conditions*.

- **Parchment Review**: Give it a read, or a skim, or just scroll to the bottom.
- **Seal the Agreement**: Click "Agree" to honor the sea's code.

6. Crafting Your Captain's Log: Creating a Computer Account

This logbook is crucial. It is where you will jot down tales of your digital travels.

- **Name Your Chronicle**: Input your name and choose a username.
- **Guard Your Tales**: Set a memorable, yet sturdy password and hint. This keeps pirates at bay!

7. Fine-tuning Your Vessel: Personalizing Settings

As you would adjust the sails and decks, fine-tune your Mac for smoother sailing:

- **Express Set Up**: Let macOS Ventura pick the optimal settings, or
- **Custom Tailoring**: Dive in and pick individual settings, from location services to analytics.
- **Choose a Voice**: Siri, your digital first mate, is eager to converse. Pick the tone and accent that pleases your ear.
- **Notification Sound**: Set the rhythm of your ship's bells—whether it is the gentle jingle of incoming messages or the triumphant blare of task completions.

8. Anchoring Down: Final Touches

With the main setup done, you are almost ready to set sail!

- **iCloud & Storage**: Decide if you wish to store your maps and treasures on iCloud.
- **Siri**: Will you have the chirpy assistant Siri aboard? You decide!

7.1 Manual Configuration on macOS Ventura

Manual Configuration on macOS Ventura is much like being the captain of your own ship, deciding the winds to follow, and the routes to chart, without an autopilot nudging you in a pre-set direction.

1. System Preferences

Ventura's 'System Preferences' is your treasure chest of controls, much like the captain's quarters in a grand ship. Herein, you will find the tools and trinkets to tweak Ventura to your liking.

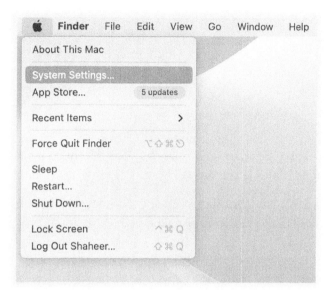

- **Dock & Menu Bar**: Adjust the size and position of your dock, much like adjusting the sails for a smoother sail. Decide which tools and apps you want nearby, and which can be stowed away.

2. Network Settings

In the digital age, our connection is our compass.

- **Wi-Fi**: Venture into 'Network' and then 'Wi-Fi', where you can manually add or forget networks, much like marking favored ports on a map or avoiding treacherous waters.

- **Advanced Settings**: For those who truly wish to dive deep, the 'Advanced' button uncovers deeper currents like DNS, Proxies, and TCP/IP configurations.

3. Display Adjustments

Every captain prefers how they view their maps and stars. In Ventura, this translates to adjusting the brightness, color, and even the arrangement of multiple screens.

- **Resolution and Display**: Whether you prefer to see the finer details or have everything appear bold and large, the 'Display' section lets you set your visual course.

4. Sound Settings

Our digital world has its own symphony. And much like a sailor tuning into the whispers of the ocean, you can tweak the soundscape of Ventura.

- **Output and Input Volume**: Balance the volume of the external world and your own voice. Be it a video call with grandchildren or listening to the golden melodies of yesteryear, ensure each sound is exactly right.

5. Security & Privacy

Every treasure chest needs a lock. And in the vast digital ocean, it is essential to ensure your ship is protected from pirates.

- **General Settings**: Set a password, decide on the duration of inactivity before your Mac locks itself. It is your digital padlock.

- **Privacy**: Control which apps can access your location, contacts, and more. Like deciding who gets to come aboard your ship.

7.2 Open and Save Files

Finding Files

Ventura's *Spotlight* is your personal detective, always ready to chase down the file of which you are thinking. Just as one would summon a genie with a rub of a lamp, simply press **Cmd + Space** and type the name of your elusive file. And voila! Your file appears, much like a star making its way onto the dance floor.

Checking out the macOS Folder Structure

Much like the grand chambers and hallways of a mansion, macOS Ventura boasts a structured folder system.

- **Finder** is your personal butler, showing you around. The *sidebar* on the left is the roadmap, showcasing destinations like *Documents*, *Downloads*, and *Pictures*.

- **Home Folder**: Represented by a little house icon, this is your personal suite in the Ventura mansion. A place where all your files feel right at home.

Saving Your Document Before It is Too Late

Imagine painting a masterpiece and then accidentally spilling water over it. Heartbreaking, right? Well, in the digital realm, we save our masterpieces.

- **Command + S**: This magical combination is the swift movement of a dancer, ensuring that your work is captured in time. It is the quick save!

- **File Menu**: Heading up to the File option on the top bar and selecting 'Save' is the more deliberate, traditional waltz step. Here, you can name your file, choose where it lives, and set its format.

Opening Icons

Icons are the honored guests in our macOS ballroom. They represent apps, files, folders, and more.

- **Double-click**: The courteous way of saying, "May I have this dance?" to an icon. A quick double tap, and the file graciously opens to you.

- **Right-click (or Ctrl + click)**: Imagine this as a gentle whisper to the icon, asking, "What can we do together?" A menu pops up, offering a range of actions, including the coveted 'Open.'

7.3 File and Folder Management

1. Setting the Stage: Getting Organized with Folders

Think of folders as the dance stages. Each set for a different act, a unique ballet. By segmenting your files into appropriate folders—whether by theme, date, or type—you are laying the foundation for a well-organized and flawless performance.

2. Crafting the Stage: Create a Folder

On your desktop or within Finder, perform a gentle right-click, then select 'New Folder.' Give it a name of your choice!

Head to the top, and from the 'File' menu, scroll down to 'New Folder.' It is classic and always elegant.

3. The Waltz of Files: Moving Around Files and Folders

Grab a file or folder with a click-and-hold, then gracefully slide it to its new location, much like a waltzing dancer gliding across the stage.

Tip: Select multiple files by holding down the **Command** key and clicking each desired file or folder.

4. The Duet: Merging Two Folders with the Same Name

When two dancers perform in harmony, it is a duet. When two folders wish to merge, macOS Ventura makes it an elegant affair.

- Drag one folder over another with the same name. A prompt appears: "A folder with the name 'X' already exists. Do you want to merge them?"

- Choose **Merge**. The two folders join seamlessly in a harmonious ballet of bytes.

5. Rename Files, Folders, and Disks

Tap once on the file or folder, wait, and tap again. The name now waits for your new name. Type away!

Right-click the file, folder, or disk, and dance down to the 'Rename' option.

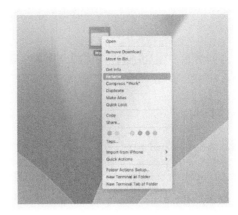

6. Delete Files and Folders

- **Drag & Drop**: Like a bow at the end of a performance, drag your file or folder to the Trash in the dock. A gracious exit.

- **Command + Delete**: A swift gesture, sending files straight to the wings (or the Trash).

7. The Grand iCloud Finale: Store Files in iCloud Drive

iCloud Drive is like a grand theater where all your files can perform globally.

- Navigate to **Finder**.

- On the sidebar, select **iCloud Drive**.

- Within this space, conduct your process—add files, create new folders, or move items around. Everything gets an encore on all your Apple devices.

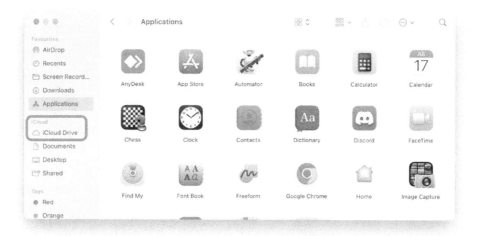

8 Apps born in iOS

iOS birthed some meaningful change apps that not only made iPhones gleam but eventually found their way onto the bigger stage of macOS Ventura. Here is a look at five of those app gems that made the grand leap, ensuring that seniors, like any other person, can enjoy the best of both Apple worlds.

1. Stocks: From Pocket Brokers to Desktop Dealers

Origins: Stocks started their journey in the snug corners of iPhones, serving as our mini stockbrokers, constantly updating with market shifts.

Mac's Take: On macOS Ventura, Stocks grew into a full-fledged stock market analyst. It provides richer charts, curated news specific to your portfolio, and an expansive view of the market. For the discerning senior, keeping track of market investments is now a breeze, all while sipping morning coffee.

2. News: Your Morning Paper Goes Digital

Origins: The News app in iOS handpicked the latest stories, turning iPhones into personalized newsstands.

Mac's Take: The migration to macOS Ventura means a more magazine-like layout on a larger canvas. The crisp and clear articles, bright images, and the intuitive categorization make it easier than ever for seniors to stay updated without squinting at tiny phone screens.

3. Voice Memos: Your Pocket-sized Recorder

Origins: Ever had a thought but no paper? iOS's Voice Memos was the quick-draw solution to recording those flashes of inspiration.

Mac's Take: On the Mac, Voice Memos takes a grander stage. With an easy-to-use interface, it is simpler for seniors to record, listen, and organize their thoughts, lectures, or even those cherished family stories for posterity.

4. Shortcuts App: The Magician's Wand

Origins: iOS introduced us to Shortcuts, the magician that turned lengthy tasks into one-tap wonders.

Mac's Take: The magic expands on macOS Ventura. Now, with a wider canvas, seniors can effortlessly automate tasks, from sending out birthday emails to organizing photos, all with a simple command. It is like having a personal assistant!

5. Home App: Command Central for Your Dwelling

Origins: On the iPhone, the home app transformed our devices into smart home maestros, controlling everything from lights to thermostats.

Mac's Take: With macOS Ventura, the Home app evolves into a command center. The larger screen offers seniors a comprehensive view of their home's smart devices, making it easier to set scenes, automate routines, or just turn off that annoying downstairs light.

9 Essential apps to chat and email

Amidst the sea of applications and software available, we find solace in some golden tools that not only connect us with our loved ones but also with the world. In this age of digital revolution, communication is paramount, and the right tool can work wonders. Let us dive into one of the gems: **WhatsApp**.

9.1 WhatsApp: A Digital Messenger Pigeon

What It Is:
WhatsApp is like the old-school messenger pigeon, just on digital steroids! It is an app that lets you send messages, make voice and video calls, and share documents and media—all without any SMS fees. Encrypted end-to-end, it offers both security and a distinctive touch, making it a favorite among many, young and old alike.

Adding WhatsApp to Your Mac: A Breeze of Installation

Step-by-Step Installation:

1. **Open Safari** (or any preferred browser) on your Mac.

2. Go to the official WhatsApp website and select **"Download"** from the menu.

3. Click on **"Download for macOS"**.

4. Once the download is complete, locate the file (usually in the Downloads folder) and open the **.dmg** file.

5. Drag the WhatsApp icon into your Applications folder.

6. Launch it from the Applications folder or through Spotlight.

Starting Fresh: Creating Your WhatsApp Account

Getting Your Account Set Up:

1. Open the WhatsApp application on your Mac.

2. A QR code will be displayed on the screen. Do not worry; it is part of the process.

3. On your mobile device, open WhatsApp.

4. Tap on the three dots on the top right corner (or settings on iPhone) and select **"WhatsApp Web/Desktop."**

5. Using your phone, scan the QR code displayed on your Mac's screen.

6. Voila! Your WhatsApp messages will now be mirrored on your Mac, allowing for easier typing and file sharing.

Using WhatsApp: A Chat Journey

Getting the Hang of It:

1. **Starting a Chat:** On the left side, click on the chat bubble icon. Select a contact and start typing!

2. **Making Calls:** Although the desktop version does not support direct calls, you can easily start a chat and switch to your phone for voice or video calls.

3. **Sharing Files:** In an open chat, click on the paperclip icon. Choose a file from your Mac and send it.

4. **Managing Chats:** Right-click on any chat to archive, pin, or mute it. This can help in keeping those important family chats at the top!

5. **Status Updates:** While more popular among the younger crowd, you can view status updates of your contacts by clicking on the circular icon next to the chat bubble.

We have previously explored the world of WhatsApp, but that is just the tip of the messaging iceberg. Beyond it lies another powerful, feature-rich, and rapidly expanding communication titan: **Telegram**. Let us journey into the realms of this app, understanding its essence, installation, and usage.

9.2 Telegram: The Blue Messenger of the Digital Era

What It Is:
Ever imagined a messenger that melds speed, security, and a slew of innovative features into one? That is Telegram for you. This cloud-based messenger allows users to send messages, voice notes, videos, and documents in a blink, all while prioritizing your privacy. With its distinctive blue theme and paper airplane logo, Telegram ensures your messages are delivered not just with speed, but with style.

Tele-Installing Telegram on Your macOS Ventura: It is a Walk in the Digital Park

Step-by-Step Installation:

1. **Launch the App Store** on your Mac.

2. Use the search bar to type in **"Telegram"**.

3. Click on **"Get"** and then **"Install"**. If prompted, enter your Apple ID password.

4. Wait a few moments for the app to download and automatically install.

5. Once installed, click **"Open"** or locate Telegram in your Applications folder and double-click to launch.

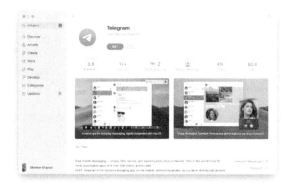

Crafting Your Telegram Persona: Account Creation

Embarking on the Telegram Journey:

1. After launching Telegram, the app will prompt you to **enter your phone number**. This is the primary identifier for your account.

2. A **verification code** will be sent to the number you provided. Enter this code in the space provided.

3. Set your **first name**, **last name**, and optionally, a **profile picture**.

4. Congratulations! You are now officially a Telegram user.

Unfurling the Telegram Tapestry: How to Use It

Mastering the Art of Telegram:

1. **Initiating a Chat:** Click on the pencil icon in the top right. Select a contact from your list or search by name.

2. **Joining Groups and Channels:** Telegram is renowned for its groups and broadcast channels. To join, click on a shared link or use the search function.

3. **Sending Files:** In an open chat, click on the paperclip icon on the bottom right. You can send anything from documents to music.

4. **Voice and Video Calls:** Click on a contact's name, and you will find icons for voice and video calls on the top right. A quality chat experience awaits!

5. **Stickers and GIFs:** Express yourself vividly! Click on the emoji icon in the chat bar, and you will find a world of animated stickers and GIFs.

6. **Privacy Settings:** Click on "Settings" (bottom right), then "Privacy and Security". Here you can manage who sees your last seen, profile photo, and more.

9.3 Messenger: More Than Just Messages

Messenger. Recognized by its iconic blue chat bubble, this application is not just any messenger – it is a portal to the world of Facebook and a treasure trove of memories, connections, and engagements.

What It Is:
Messenger, owned by Facebook, is not just your regular messaging app. It is a universe where text chats, video calls, group conversations, and multimedia sharing converge. Add to that the ability to send stickers, play games, and even make payments in some regions, and you have yourself a multi-functional communication powerhouse. With the signature 'ding' notification, every message brings you closer to someone, somewhere in the world.

Welcoming Messenger to Your macOS Ventura

The Installation Voyage:

1. **Launch the App Store**: Begin by accessing the App Store on your Mac.

2. **Search for the Star**: In the search bar, key in **"Messenger"**.

3. **Install with a Click**: Find the official Messenger app, recognizable by its blue chat bubble icon. Tap on **"Get"** followed by **"Install"**. If needed, verify with your Apple ID credentials.

4. **Ring the Bell**: Once the app has comfortably nestled into your Mac, either click **"Open"** or find Messenger in your Applications folder and double-click to awaken it.

Stepping Into the Messenger Universe: Account Creation

Your Messenger Passport:

1. If you are already a citizen of Facebook, rejoice! Your passport is ready. Use your **Facebook credentials** to log in.

2. For the uninitiated, click on **"Create New Account"**. This will redirect you to a browser for a full sign-up process on Facebook. Remember, your Facebook and Messenger accounts are interlinked.

Navigating the Constellations of Conversations: How to Use Messenger

Your Map to Mastering Messenger:

1. **Ping a Pal**: Click on the pencil and pad icon to initiate a new chat. Choose a contact and let the conversation flow!

2. **Virtual Face-to-Face**: Eyeing a more personal connection? Click on the video icon on the top right corner of a chat to dive into a video call.

3. **From Your Fellowship**: To create a group chat, click on the 'Groups' tab on the left, then select 'Create a New Group'. Add members, pick a fun name, and even a quirky group photo!

4. **Express with Flair**: Use GIFs, stickers, emojis, and more by clicking on the four-dot icon beside the chat typing space.

5. **Venture Beyond Text**: Attach photos, videos, or documents by clicking on the paperclip icon in the chat box.

6. **Dive into Settings**: Click on your profile icon on the top left to access settings. Customize notifications, privacy settings, or even switch to dark mode for a nocturnal chat ambiance.

9.4   Snapchat: A Glimpse into the Ephemeral

What It Is:
Snapchat is like a digital masquerade ball. You share photos and videos, known as "Snaps", with your friends, but there is a twist: they disappear after being viewed! With creative filters, stickers, and Bitmoji integrations, every Snap is an art piece waiting to be crafted. Beyond this, the "Stories" feature lets you string together multiple Snaps for a 24-hour showcase, and "Discover" immerses you in a sea of content from friends, celebrities, and brands.

Setting Sail with Snapchat on Your macOS Ventura

Embarking on the Installation Odyssey:

1. **Begin at the Dock**: Navigate to the App Store, the gateway to a myriad of digital wonders.

2. **Seek the Ghost**: In the search bar, type **"Snapchat"**. Look out for the iconic yellow icon with a ghost.

3. **Anchor it Down**: Click on **"Get"** and then **"Install"**. You might need to authenticate using your Apple ID.

4. **Unmask the Spirit**: Once installed, you will spot the playful ghost of Snapchat in your Applications folder. Double-click to bring it to life.

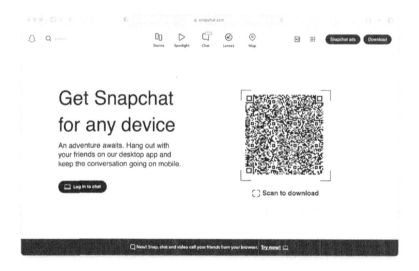

Crafting Your Snapchat Persona: Account Creation

Carving Your Identity:

1. Launch the app and tap **"Sign Up"**.

2. Share your birthday (it is crucial for age-specific features), choose a unique username, and craft a password.

3. Input your email or mobile number for verification and viola! Your Snapchat persona is ready.

Navigating the Ever-Changing Waters of Snapchat: How to Use

Your Map to the Ephemeral Realm:

1. **Capture a Snap**: Click the circular button at the bottom to snap a picture. Hold it for a video. Release to end.

2. **Artistry Unleashed**: Swipe left or right to explore filters. Tap the sticker icon for Bitmojis, timestamps, and more.

3. **Pen Down Thoughts**: Click the 'T' icon and type your message. Play around with color and size.

4. **Send Your Snap**: Tap the blue arrow, select friends, and off your Snap goes, disappearing once viewed!

5. **Narrate Your Day**: To add your Snap to Stories, click on the square+ icon next to the blue arrow. Your story lasts 24 hours.

6. **Engage and Explore**: Swipe left to chat and right to explore the Discover page. Dive deep and let curiosity be your guide.

9.5 Messages Application

The design of the Messages app has not been significantly updated, but there have been additions made to the app that users have been requesting for years. It is possible to edit an iMessage for up to 15 minutes after it has been sent using the edit option, and there is also the option to unsend any message for up to 15 minutes after it has been sent using the same option.

Messages sent via SMS cannot be edited or resent after they have been sent; this functionality is only available for iMessages with the blue bubble. Additionally, it requires that all participants have either iOS 16 or macOS Ventura installed on their devices. If you receive a message but do not want to address it right away, you have the option of marking it as unread so that you do not forget to investigate it later. As of recently, there is also the option to recover recently deleted messages for up to 30 days after they have been deleted. This means that if you delete something by accident, it is no longer permanently lost. Within the filtered section of the Messages app, you will find any messages that you've previously deleted. Notably, an update has been made so that Messages, in addition to being compatible with FaceTime, can also work with SharePlay. You can have conversations with your friends through SharePlay while you are doing things like watching movies, listening to music, playing games, working out, using apps, and more. SharePlay is compatible with FaceTime and Messages, allowing you to collaborate with your friends and family on projects while having a conversation either through a text-based exchange or a video call. Apple has released an updated version of Memoji for use in Messages, which includes seventeen new hairstyles, additional sticker options, and updated nose options.

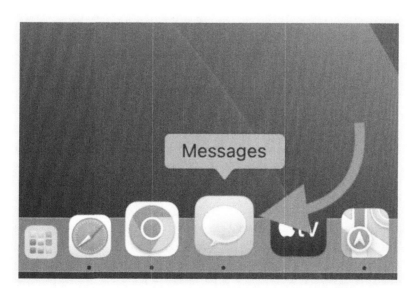

9.6 Mail

Apple made a number of changes to the Mail app in macOS Ventura to bring it closer in line with other third-party email applications. If you send an email in error, there are tools that allow you to retract the message within ten seconds, and there is also the option to schedule messages to be sent later. If you are unable to immediately respond to an email message, you have the option to receive a reminder to do so through the Remind Me feature.

Undo Send

This is the most useful function that can be found in any email client or email service. Do not worry if you accidentally sent an email to the wrong person, made a typo in the subject line, sent it to the wrong recipient, forgot to attach a file to it, or anything else like that. You have a brief window of time within the Mail app in macOS Ventura to reverse the sending of the email and retrieve it. When you send an email, the Undo Send option is displayed in the interface of the app in the area near the bottom left corner. You have a delay of about ten seconds, during which time you have the option available to you. This will prevent the email from being sent by removing it from the outbox and saving it in the folder designated for drafts on your computer. That gives you the opportunity to correct your errors.

Apple has not only included the unsend feature in the Mail app but also in the Messages app, and it will be available in iOS 16 as well. The feature is not unique to the Mail app.

Scheduled Send

When you have finished composing an email, there are times when you might decide against sending it right away. It is a special message wishing someone on their birthday or anniversary, or it is late at night, or it is the weekend, and you do not want to disturb your contact. Whatever the case may be, you do not want to interrupt them. When this occurs, the function known as Scheduled Sends kicks into gear. You can choose when you want the message to be sent by clicking the drop-down menu that is located next to the Send button and selecting either "Tonight," "Tomorrow," or "at a Specific Date and Time of Your Choice." You can examine the messages that you have planned to send later by selecting the Send Later tab located on the app's sidebar.

Smarter mailbox

The Mail app now has support for Rich Links, which allows for the presentation of a thumbnail preview of the contents of a web page. If you copy a link and then paste it into the mail composer, rather than seeing an uninteresting text link, you will see the content of the link directly in the message. It is remarkably like what we see in most instant messaging apps available today but having it in the email client is a welcome addition. If you want to get rid of a link, click the X button that is located inside the preview. After you do that, the app will use the text version of the URL. Simply click the thumbnail button that is located at the very end of the link to re-add it. If you click the send mail button in Apple's Mail app without first including a recipient in a thread, the app will ask you to include them in the message. The application will give you a warning about it if your email indicates that you are sending a file, but there are no documents or media attached to the message. You have the option of ignoring the warning or clicking the "Don't Send" button, after which you can attach the file and send it.

Follow-Up

If you send an email to someone but do not receive a response, you might want to follow up with them by giving them a friendly nudge in the form of a reminder. What happens, though, if you do not remember to do that? You have the option within the Mail app to pin previously sent messages to the top of your inbox, which will make it easier for you to follow up on them. According to Apple, the application will offer automatic suggestions if you do not receive a response to an email.

Remind Me

If you find that after reading a message you want to return to it later, the Mail app allows you to explicitly set a reminder for yourself in case you forget about it. Simply choose an email and then right-click on it to activate the feature. Simply select one of the following options from the Remind Me menu after clicking on it: Don't forget to remind me in 1 hour, tonight, or tomorrow, or you can always do it later. The final choice gives you the ability to set the reminder for a particular time and day of the week. The Mail app will notify you to check the message after the allotted amount of time has passed. The "Remind Me" label will appear on any messages that have been flagged by the feature. Through the "Remind Me" tab located in the sidebar, you will have speedy access to the messages.

Search

The search function in the Mail app is both quicker and more accurate than it was in the past. The Mail app now provides a richer view of content from the moment a search is initiated, which allows the Mail app to anticipate what you might want to look for when you search. In addition to helping, you find what you are looking for, Search will also search for synonyms of the words you enter and correct any typos it finds. If you have not received a response to a message that you have sent, the Mail app can bring an email that you have already sent to the top of your inbox so that you are reminded to follow up with the recipient. It is possible for the Mail app to remind you if you forget to include an attachment or a recipient who is copied on the message. Mail now supports rich links, giving more context to web links and other information that may be included in email messages. This feature was previously only available in Messages.

9.7 Gmail: Unveiling the E-Pigeon

What It Is:

Gmail is Google's flagship email service, serving over a billion people worldwide. Think of it as your digital mailbox where you can send, receive, and organize emails. Apart from the basic mail functions, it offers spam protection, powerful search features, and integration with other Google services, making it a favorite for personal and professional communication.

Inviting Gmail onto Your macOS Ventura

Charting Your Installation Course:

1. **Commence at the Dock**: Direct your cursor to the App Store, the hub of digital marvels.

2. **Seek the Red 'M'**: Punch in **"Gmail"** in the search bar. The red 'M' signifies the digital postman's presence.

3. **Anchor Gmail Down**: Hit **"Get"** followed by **"Install"**. Your Apple ID might request your attention for authentication.

4. **Roll Out the Red Carpet**: Post-installation, the illustrious red 'M' will reside in your Applications folder. Give it a click to open your digital mailbox.

Crafting Your Digital Address: Account Creation

Staking Your Spot in the Digital World:

1. Launch Gmail and select **"Create account"**.

2. Provide necessary details: name, desired email address, and password.

3. Google will guide you through a few more steps, including phone number verification for added security. Upon completion, your Gmail address is set, and you are officially part of the vast Gmail universe.

Mastering the Art of Digital Letters: How to Use Gmail

Your Guide to Digital Correspondence:

1. **Penning Your Letter**: Click the vibrant '+ Compose' button. It is like summoning your digital parchment.

2. **Address and Content**: Enter the recipient's email in 'To'. Craft your subject and dive into the body of your message.

3. **Attachments and Embellishments**: Want to attach photos or documents? The paperclip icon is your ally. Emojis? The smiley face beckons.

4. **Send Off Your Pigeon**: Once satisfied, hit the 'Send' button. Your digital pigeon is off!

5. **Organizing**: Drag and drop emails into folders or label them as you see fit. An organized mailbox is a happy mailbox.

6. **Search Magic**: Looking for an old email? The search bar atop is equipped with Google's powerful search magic.

10   Videocalls

In an era where the world feels more connected than ever, video calls have become the new coffee catchup, and macOS Ventura ensures that seniors are not left behind. Let us explore the video call features that this OS has to offer.

Use of the Camera

Before we dive deep into video calling, it is essential to understand the basics of the macOS Ventura camera settings.

Settings: Go to System Preferences > Security & Privacy > Camera to ensure apps you wish to use have permission to access the camera.

Adjusting Image Quality: To get the best out of your camera, ensure your surroundings are well lit. The brighter the environment, the clearer you will appear on the call.

Capturing Moments: Photo & Video

Taking a Snapshot: While on a video call, there might be moments you want to freeze. Use the camera's snapshot or screenshot feature, typically represented by a camera icon, to capture that precious moment.

Recording a Video: Some apps allow you to record entire sessions. Look for a red dot or a 'Record' button. Remember, it is always polite to ask for permission before recording!

Filters and Effects

Feeling playful? Ventura's camera compatibility with numerous apps allows users to try on various filters, from subtle touch-ups to whimsical effects that transport you to outer space or give you bunny ears! Just search for the 'Effects' or 'Filters' tab in your video calling app and let the fun begin.

Mastering Zoom

Zoom has become the darling of video conferencing, and understanding its basics is essential:

- **Joining a Meeting**: Click on the link provided, or open the Zoom app and enter the meeting ID.

- **Mute/Unmute**: Found at the bottom left corner, this button controls your microphone.

- **Start/Stop Video**: Right next to the mute button, control your camera with this option.

- **Gallery View/Speaker View**: Choose how you wish to see participants - either as a grid or focus on the person speaking.

QR Codes: The Modern Magic Carpet

QR codes are those little square barcodes you see everywhere these days. They act as portals to transport you directly to websites, videos, or even video calls.

Scanning a QR code with macOS Ventura:

1. Open 'Camera' on your Mac.

2. Point the camera to the QR code. Make sure the code is clearly visible in the camera view.

3. A notification will pop up, indicating what action the QR code will lead to.

4. Click on the notification to complete the action, whether it is joining a video call, visiting a website, or watching a video.

To wrap up, while video calling might seem like the realm of the tech-savvy youth, macOS Ventura's intuitive design ensures seniors can join in with ease. So, set that camera angle right, pick a fun filter if that is your style, and hop on a video call to share stories, laughter, and memories. Happy calling!

10.1 Facetime

How to Set Up FaceTime

It is simple to make a video or voice call using FaceTime. A built-in or linked microphone and camera are all that is required, along with a broadband internet connection.

Setting up FaceTime

You do not need to download anything else since the FaceTime program is already installed on your Mac, and the setup is simple:

1. Click the **FaceTime icon** on the menu bar to launch the FaceTime application, or **press ⌘ + Space and enter FaceTime**.

2. To activate FaceTime, click **Turn On** if it is not already.

3. Enter your Apple ID and password to log in.

4. Navigate to **FaceTime > Preferences** to choose how and by whom you may be accessed on FaceTime. You can choose here whether you wish to use FaceTime with all the email addresses associated with your Apple account (for example, you might not want people who have your work email address to contact you this way).

5. Uncheck any email addresses that you do not want to be associated with FaceTime calls to you.

6. Simply visit **System Settings > Apple ID > Name, Phone, Email > Reachable** and click the + symbol to add an email address to the list. The modifications will immediately show up in FaceTime settings.

How to call someone on FaceTime

FaceTime for Mac is simple to use as long as both you and the person you are calling have a strong internet connection, are signed in, and have the software open:

1. Open the **Contacts app**.

2. Look up the individual you want to call. A name, phone number, or email address may be used to search.

3. Select the option to initiate a FaceTime call by clicking on the contact's profile (looks like a video camera icon).

4. Making a FaceTime call is now easier due to shared links. To invite individuals, click **New FaceTime** once you have opened FaceTime and enter their phone numbers or email addresses. Alternatively, choose "**Create a Link**" to send it to anybody.

How to accept calls using FaceTime

The steps:

1. First, a pop-up window will appear. You will see a notification in the upper-right area if FaceTime has been closed.

2. If you have the caller's information in the Contacts app, the notice will let you know who is calling.

3. Click **Accept** if you want to communicate with them.

4. If you get a FaceTime link, you can join by clicking the link.

5. Click the **red handset symbol** to hang up the call.

What does the group FaceTime entail?

Group FaceTime is for situations when you need to collect several people, such as a family reunion or business conference. Up to thirty-two users can participate in a single active video conversation on the FaceTime app.

To place a group FaceTime call:

1. Launch the **FaceTime app** and choose **"New FaceTime."**

2. Type the contact information—name, phone number, or email address—of each person you want to FaceTime in a group, separated by commas. Alternatively, choose each one from your Contacts separately.

3. To start the group FaceTime video conference, click the **green video icon.**

4. To invite extra people to a Group FaceTime session that is already in progress, click in the lower-left corner of the window to reveal the sidebar, click **Add Person** to enter their details, and then pick **Add.**

5. When someone joins a group FaceTime chat, their videos will show up as identically sized tiles in a grid layout. One's title gets highlighted while they are speaking. The Portrait mode (click your **tile > Video Effects**) might also be useful.

How to Stop Unwanted FaceTime Calls?

If you would want, FaceTime lets you quickly ban any caller at any time:

The steps:

1. Start FaceTime.

2. Use your Apple ID to log in.

3. Look up the caller you want to ban specifically.

4. Right-click on a number and select **Block This Caller.**

Use FaceTime Links

FaceTime links allow you to transmit a link to every participant before the conversation starts, making it simpler to prepare for FaceTime calls. You may invite friends who use Android and Windows phones to call using FaceTime Links. When using the most recent version of Chrome or Edge, you can use the link to join from their browser.

The steps:

1. On your Mac, launch the **FaceTime application.**

2. To access the sharing menu, click **Create Link** . The link can then be copied, or you can choose another sharing method.

3. After generating the connection, it displays in the FaceTime window's sidebar.

4. Double-click the FaceTime Link in the sidebar or click the FaceTime icon next to it to initiate the call. Click the Join button after that.

5. Other people need to be allowed to join the call when they access the FaceTime link and click **Join.**

- Select the checkbox next to their name to allow them to join the call.

- Click the Decline button ⊗ next to their name to reject their invitation to join the call.

- After they have joined, click the delete button ⊗ within 30 seconds to cut them off from the call.

    6. Click the Info button ⓘ in the sidebar next to the link, then click **Delete Link**, to remove a FaceTime link. When a link is deleted, you are no longer informed whenever someone clicks on it, and anybody who does view it merely sees that they are awaiting authorization.

    7. In the Calendar app, a connection can also be made. When creating a new event, choose FaceTime by clicking the FaceTime icon next to **"Add Location or Video Call."** Everyone you invite will be aware of the precise location and time of the meeting thanks to the smooth FaceTime connection integration with the Calendar event.

    ### Join a Call Using a FaceTime Link

The steps:

    1. Select the **FaceTime option**. The link opens on your web browser if you are using a device that cannot access it in the FaceTime app. The most recent versions of Microsoft Edge and Google Chrome both enable FaceTime connections on Android and Windows devices.

    2. To join the call through a web browser, you must first enter your name to do so. Click **Continue** after that.

    3. Select **Join**, then wait to be allowed in.

11   Create a document

In the golden age of technology, pens and paper metamorphose into digital canvases and keys. MacOS Ventura unfolds an intuitive bridge between the analog world and the digital realm, making it a breeze for seniors to craft, shape, and share their stories, thoughts, plans, and memories. Here are the steps of document creation!

11.1 The Beginning: Choosing Your App

The greatness of macOS Ventura lies in its myriad applications designed for diverse types of creations:

- **TextEdit**: Your trusty old diary, but digital! Ideal for jotting down memories, crafting letters, or even drafting an agenda for the next family reunion.

- **Pages**: Think of this as your elegant writing desk where you pen down stories, design newsletters for the local club, or even create beautiful birthday cards for the grandkids.

- **Numbers**: The modern ledger, perfect for maintaining budgets, tracking the backyard bird count, or planning the next big family event.

- **Keynote**: Your stage to shine, where you can stitch together photos, memories, and notes to share at gatherings or teach a thing or two to the younger ones.

Taking the First Step:

1. Click on the **Finder** icon in your dock (that happy face at the bottom) and navigate to the **Applications** folder.

2. Find and open your chosen application, be it TextEdit, Pages, Numbers, or Keynote.

3. Once inside, you will be greeted with an array of template options. Feel free to choose one or start with a blank slate.

4. Look for the **'New Document'** option. If it is a tad elusive, journey to the top menu and select **File > New**.

Crafting with Flair:

Once you have started, the world is your oyster! Use the top menu to:

- Add images by choosing **Insert > Choose**, letting you pull in that lovely picture of your garden.

- Play with text styles, colors, and sizes to add that distinctive touch.

- Insert tables, charts, or even links by using the **Insert** menu.

11.2 Formatting Documents

Ah, the art of writing! In the time of Shakespeare, the quill danced on parchment. Now, in the era of macOS Ventura, we have a plethora of tools at our fingertips to craft digital masterpieces. But fear is not! While the tools have changed, the heart of storytelling remains the same. Here is a burst of wisdom on how to give your documents that extra polish in macOS Ventura.

Dressed in the Best Font:

Your words deserve to be dressed in the finest:

Fonts & Styles: Think of these as the unique clothing for your text. In your document:

- Choose **Format > Show Fonts** or **Format > Font > Show Fonts**.

- From the glorious list that emerges, select the font that resonates with your mood.

- You can also delve into **Format > Style** to add boldness, italics, or underline to your text.

Splash of Color:

Add vibrancy to your words:

Colors: Envision your document as a canvas:

- Go to **Format > Show Colors** or **Format > Font > Show Colors**.

- Like choosing the paint for a masterpiece, select a color that captures the essence of your sentiment.

Exquisite Characters:

- For those times when English just does not cut it, and you want to add a little 'je ne sais quoi' to your text:

- Easily add characters with accent marks or diacritic touches, making your text truly global.

The Guardian of Grammar:

Never let a typo cloud your message:

- **Spell Check**: Ventura's got your back!

  - While you are immersed in writing, the system diligently checks your spelling.

  - Should it spot an error, it will gently underline it, like a friend whispering a suggestion.

  - If auto-correction is not your cup of tea, navigate to **Preferences** and adjust to your comfort.

The Power of Knowledge:

When in doubt, seek wisdom:

- **Definitions**: Ever stumble upon a word that feels like an enigma?

  - Simply highlight the word, Control-click it, and choose **Look Up**.

  - Lo and behold! The definition gracefully appears.

- **Translation**: Share your tales with the world.

  - Highlight the text, Control-click, and choose **Translate**. Within moments, your words are ready to touch hearts across borders.

11.3 Saving Your Masterpiece

After pouring your thoughts and memories into the document:

1. Click **File** in the top menu.

2. Select **Save**.

3. Choose a memorable name, select where you would like to keep it, and press **Save**.

The exhilaration of writing, capturing thoughts, pouring one's soul onto the canvas of the virtual page. But what happens when the power goes out, or the mischievous cat walks over your keyboard? The horror! Worry not. Just as ancient scrolls preserved tales of yore, macOS Ventura provides modern tools to safeguard your digital masterpieces. Let us dive into the craft of saving:

Auto-Save

- macOS Ventura, like a diligent scribe, often **saves your documents automatically** as you are pouring out your thoughts.

- Feel secure, knowing that Ventura has your back, guarding your creations from unexpected disruptions.

Taking the Reins: Manual Save

- While Ventura works its magic in the background, there is the charm of saving manually, to immortalize a moment.

  - In your document, head to **File > Save**.

  - A prompt emerges, waiting for you to christen your work with a name.

- Choose your location to save. Should you wish to explore more hideouts for your document, click the down arrow button.

- Click **Save**.

Tags: The Compass in Digital Seas

- As you save, consider adorning your document with **tags**. These function as beacons, guiding you to your documents when the digital sea gets stormy.

Cloud's Embrace: iCloud Drive

- Consider entrusting your document to the vast skies of **iCloud Drive**. Here, it not only rests secure but also dances across your Apple devices, making it available wherever you go.

A New Identity: Save As

- Ever had a fresh perspective and wished to save a variation of your document?

    - Go to **File > Save As**.

    - If 'Save As' does not appear, simply hold the magical **Option key**, and the path reveals itself.

    - Give your work a new identity, a new name.

Cloning Masterpieces: Duplicate

- Why not have two of something good? Clone your masterwork with **File > Duplicate** or venture again into **File > Save As**.

The Art of Sharing: PDFs

- Sometimes, sharing means encapsulating your document in the universal embrace of a **PDF**.

- And if you are feeling particularly adventurous, bind multiple tales into a singular PDF anthology.

- Open your document

- Select File > Print

- Press the PDF button or down arrow which reveals PDF pop-up menu. Select Save as PDF

- Select location and give it a name

- You may add a password to your document by going to Security Options

12   Manage the music

In the quiet of a room, or amid the hustle and bustle of daily life, music is always around our hearts. With macOS Ventura, this symphony is not just about listening; it is about orchestrating your music collection with flair and ease. So, are you ready to wield your baton and manage your melodies?

12.1 The Musical Archive: The Music App

- Think of the **Music App** on macOS Ventura as the grand library of Alexandria, but for songs. Every note, every beat, stored and catalogued for your listening pleasure.

Importing New Melodies: Adding Songs

- Found an old CD or a digital collection you wish to add?

    - Simply **drag and drop** your tunes into Music App or choose **File > Add to Library**. Like welcoming a guest musician into an orchestra, Ventura makes the integration seamless.

Crafting Your Setlists: Playlists

- Whether it is 'Golden Oldies' or 'Rainy Day Melodies,' create **playlists** that match your mood.

    - Click on the **"+"** at the bottom left, name your playlist, and drag in your chosen tracks. Every day can have its soundtrack.

Ventura's Recommendations: Genius Playlists

- Let macOS Ventura be your musical sommelier, crafting playlists from songs in your library that go great together. Activate **Genius Playlists**, and Ventura shall surprise you!

The Grand Stage: Playing Your Music

- Double-click on a track and let the magic flow. Use the playback controls to play, pause, skip, or rewind. Slide the volume control for a gentle lullaby or a grand crescendo.

Delving into Details: Editing Song Info

- From the era of Beethoven to the age of Rock, every piece has its story.

    - **Right-click** on a track and choose **Song Info**. Here, you can edit details, add artwork, or pen down lyrics. Like a music historian, you get to chronicle each note's journey.

The Grand Farewell: Deleting Tracks

- As with any ensemble, sometimes a piece no longer fits.

    - **Right-click** on a song and select **Delete from Library**. The piece takes a bow and exits gracefully, but the memories linger.

Universal Access: Sync with iCloud

- Your musical treasure is not bound by the four walls of your room. With **iCloud**, your music roams free, echoing across all your Apple devices. Set up **iCloud Music Library** and let your symphony travel with you.

12.2 Add and Download Music

You will be able to add songs, playlists, albums, and music videos to your music library from Apple Music as soon as you sign up for Apple Music. Your music library will then be available anytime you are logged in to Music on your iPhone, iPad, Mac, or iPod touch. After adding songs to your music collection, you will have the option to download them to your computer or other devices so that you may play them at any time, even when you are not connected to the internet.

Note: The Apple Songs Voice Plan does not allow for the uploading or downloading of music. Several nations and locations do not have access to Apple Music Voice, Apple Music, Dolby Atmos, or lossless.

12.3 Add Music to your Library

The steps:

1. To locate music that you want to add to the library, open the **Music app** on Mac and do either of the below:

   - **See specific suggestions that have been made for you:** Click **Listen Now** in left sidebar, and you will access music that you have recently listened to, customized playlists that have been produced for you, genres that you may like, and other options.
   - **Check out the latest additions to Apple Music:** You can search for music based on your mood, recent releases, charts, and more by clicking the **Browse button** in the left sidebar.
   - Search the Apple Music library.

2. It is possible to add to the songs in your collection by doing one of the below:

   - To add anything, move cursor over the item you want, then click **Add button** +.
   - To add an item to your library, move the pointer over the item you want to add (for example, an album or song), press **More button** ..., and select **Add to Library**.
   - To add item to sidebar, drag it there. For example, if you drag a given song, you have the option of adding it to your library or a particular playlist instead.

Note: With the Apple Music playlist, songs in playlist become updated once the owner of the playlist alters them; however, individual songs stop displaying in your songs list. This happens when you add a playlist to your library.

3. If the above options are not available, you are either not logged in to your Apple Music with your Apple ID, you are yet to join Apple Music, or you have not chosen Sync Library option in Music preferences. To check: Select **Music > Preferences**, then click **General**. Make sure that the checkbox next to Sync Library is checked, and then press OK.

Say something like, **"Add this music to my library,"** and then wait for Siri's response.

12.4 Download Music to your Mac

The steps:

1. Launch the Music app on your Mac, and in the sidebar, choose an option that is located underneath the library heading. For instance, you can see all the songs in your collection by clicking the **Songs tab**.

2. Hover the cursor over any item, then choose one of the below to begin downloading music to your computer that you have added to your music library:

   - To download, click the icon labeled **"Download ↓."**

- To download, first, choose **More** ⋯ from the menu, then click the **Download option**.

If the song you wish to download is in Dolby Atmos, Dolby button ◗◖ will display next to it. You get the option to download the song in either stereo or Dolby Atmos format depending on your preference. Choose **Songs > Preferences**, press **General**, and then choose **Download Dolby Atmos tickbox**. This will allow you to download music in Dolby Atmos whenever it is made available.

Note that music that is downloaded from Apple Music to your personal computer cannot be manually copied onto an iOS device like an iPad, iPhone, or iPod, nor can it be physically burnt to a disc. Apple Music is the only source from which music may be downloaded straight onto a device.

12.5 Playing Songs

Ah, the pleasure of music! It is like stepping into a time machine, reliving moments, or creating brand-new ones. With macOS Ventura, you get the conductor's podium to orchestrate this symphony exactly as you wish. Let us explore this harmonious journey.

1. Waking up Siri, Your Musical Aide

Imagine a helpful assistant, always eager to spin your favorite tracks. That is Siri for you!

- **Ask her to play**: "Siri, play some music."

- **Got a specific mood or album?** "Siri, play the 'Golden Days' playlist."

- **Wondering about that catchy tune?** "Siri, what song is this?"

- **Need a pause?** "Siri, pause the song."

- **Ready for more melodies?** "Siri, resume the music."

Remember, like any maestro, Siri is there to assist, awaiting your command.

2. The Grand Musical Library

The **Music app** is your ornate music cabinet, filled with melodies new and old:

- **Seeking a specific tune or album?** Under the Library in the sidebar, click on categories like 'Albums' or 'Artists'.

- **Mood for curated lists?** Dive into your Playlists in the sidebar.

- **On a treasure hunt?** Use the search bar to find your hidden gems.

3. Playing Your Chosen Harmonies

- Hover over your song choice, and a play button appears, as if the universe knows you are about to embark on a musical journey. Click and sail away.

4. Customize Your Concert

- **Shuffle and Serendipity**: Mix things up with the shuffle feature.

- **Encores?** Set your favorite tracks on repeat.

- **Set The Sequence**: Arrange the Playing Next queue as you fancy.

- **Smooth Transitions**: Fade between songs for a seamless experience.

- **Selective Hearing**: If you wish some songs to remain silent in a playlist, just opt to prevent them from playing.

- **Feedback Matters**: Love or dislike songs to refine your musical experiences.

5. Old School Tunes: Playing from a CD

While we bask in the digital age, there's nostalgia in playing music from a CD. Insert it, and macOS Ventura gracefully understands, ready to play those classics.

12.6 Shuffling and Repeating Songs

Ever wanted to switch things up and let your music library surprise you? Or you have stumbled upon a song so good, you could listen to it on repeat for hours. With macOS Ventura's Music app, the choice is yours, and the controls are in your hands. Let us unravel the magic behind shuffling and repeating songs:

1. Siri, Your Melodious Assistant

Before we dive in, let us remember our musical assistant, Siri:

"Feeling adventurous today? Just say, **'Siri, shuffle my music,'** and let her craft a medley for you."

2. Entering the Musical Arena

To navigate the waves of your songs:

- **Tune into Apple Music**: Stream and discover a world of melodies.

- **Dive into your Personal Collection**: Play songs handpicked over time from your library.

- **Old Classics**: Pop onto your CD and ride the nostalgia.

Note: Before you start the shuffle or repeat dance, a song needs to be playing in the background.

3. Shuffling: The Unexpected Journey

- **The Universal Shuffle**: Click on the vibrant Shuffle button in the playback controls. When activated, this button lights up, sending your songs into a delightful jumble.

- **Album Adventures**: Prefer an album-centric shuffle? Choose **Controls > Shuffle > Albums**. Your Mac plays the songs in their album sequence, then picks another album to start all over.

- **Single Album Shuffle**: Hover over an album, click the **More button**, and choose **Shuffle [album name]**. Dive deep into that album's universe, with songs playing in no order.

4. Repeating: Relishing the Rhythms

- **The Loop of Songs**: Click the **Repeat button**. When it is illuminated, every song in your current view (like a playlist) will be on a loop.

- **One Song Symphony**: Can't get enough of that tune? Double-click the **Repeat button** until you see the number '1'. Now, that song is all yours, over and over.

- **Pause the Loop**: Had enough? Click the **Repeat button** until it grays out. Your musical journey returns to its regular course.

Playing Next Queue

In the realm of music, where beats collide and melodies intertwine, macOS Ventura's Music app offers you an enjoyable way of enjoying your music. With the "Playing Next Queue," you no longer must be at the mercy of a playlist. Instead, you can sculpt your upcoming song list like a maestro with a baton. Let us explore how.

1. Behind the Curtain of the Playing Next Queue

Imagine you are indulging in a serene playlist, and suddenly, you are reminded of an energetic album you would like to jam to. "Playing Next Queue" is your tool to seamlessly switch between the two. Play your favorite album and, once it concludes, the Music app will gently guide you back to your original playlist.

2. Autoplay: Your Silent DJ

For the times when you are unsure of the next musical turn, embrace the magic of **Autoplay**. Upon playing a song, the Autoplay feature curates a list of similar tunes, queuing them up for your enjoyment. The telltale sign of Autoplay at work is its distinctive icon on the Playing Next queue.

3. Commanding the Stage: Using the Playing Next Queue

Beginning the Journey: First, have a song or playlist in play. The "Playing Next" function springs to life when there's ongoing music.

Directing the Queue:

- **Autoplay Toggle**: Click the Autoplay button at the top of the queue. A change in its color signifies its activation. Turning it off on one device linked to your Apple ID ensures it is off on all of them.

- **Select Your Next Act**: Double-click any song within the queue to play it next.

- **Prioritize a Song**: Hover over your chosen song, click the **More button**, and select **Play Next** to move it to the front of the line.

- **Rearrange Your Setlist**: Simply drag and drop songs to customize their play order.

- **Removing a Song or Clearing the Stage**: Choose a song and press the Delete key to remove it. Or opt for the **Clear link** at the top to purge the entire queue.

- **Walk Down Memory Lane**: Click the **History link** to see which melodies have serenaded you recently.

To exit the queue, simply click the "Playing Next" button again.

Sort Songs

Every relevant story has a flow, a narrative arc that captures the reader's imagination. Think of your music collection in the same way: each track a chapter, each album a story arc. macOS Ventura's Music app is the tool that lets you become the storyteller of your own musical journey. Here is how you can masterfully sort your songs, crafting the rhythm of your day.

1. The Power of Voice: Siri at Your Service

You might have asked Siri for the weather or to call a friend, but have you ever commanded your musical choices with just your voice? With macOS Ventura, make Siri your personal DJ.

Command Examples:

- "Hey Siri, go to the next track."

- "Hey Siri, rewind to the start of this song."

Remember, Siri is always eager to assist, helping you streamline your musical experience.

2. The Sort Pop-up Menu: Your Musical Compass

Whether you are meticulously organized or spontaneously spirited, the Sort pop-up menu in your music library is your compass, guiding your tracks.

Steps:

1. Within the Music app, select any category under **Library** or a specific **playlist** from the sidebar.

2. Spot the Sort pop-up menu in the top-right. Here, you are presented with choices to determine your song order, from 'Time' to 'Artist Name', and 'Ascending' to 'Descending'.

3. Once sorted, simply hit the Play button, and your tunes flow seamlessly in your chosen order.

3. Click, Column, Curate!

Sometimes, you just know exactly what you are in the mood for, be it a nostalgic track from the eighties or a jazz classic. Columns are your go-to:

Steps:

1. Click on **Songs** under **Library**.

2. Spot those column headings? A single click lets you instantly sort by song title, artist, album, or other intriguing categories.

3. Dive deeper! For those with an eye for detail, navigate to **View > Show View Options**. It is like opening a treasure chest of sorting choices.

4. To set the musical stage, double-click your starter track, and let the Music app weave the rest of your auditory narrative.

13   How to share contents

Sharing is caring, and MacOS Ventura embodies this by making the sharing of files and folders easier than ever. For seniors who might feel a bit overwhelmed by technological jargon, this guide is crafted to provide a gentle walk through the park, bringing the straightforward steps to share your cherished memories, documents, and more.

Setting Up Sharing: An Introduction

Imagine having a library of memories or important documents, and you wish to share them with family or a select group of friends. MacOS Ventura's file sharing is your friendly librarian, assisting in curating and distributing the content just the way you want.

Step-by-Step Guide to File Sharing

1. **Begin the Journey**: On your Mac, navigate to the Apple menu > System Settings. Within the sidebar, find 'General' and then look to the right to click 'Sharing'. This might be slightly down, so scrolling might be necessary.

2. **Switch On Sharing**: With a simple toggle, turn on 'File Sharing'. There is an 'Info' button on the right which can provide additional details if needed.

3. **Choosing What to Share**: By default, MacOS Ventura is kind enough to share the 'Public' folder of every account on your Mac. But what if you want to share a specific memory album or document folder? Simply click the 'Add' button, find your desired folder, and add it. If you change your mind or decide against sharing something, the 'Remove' button is your friend.

4. **The Personal Touch**: Want to add a more distinctive touch? Control-click on the folder's name, go to 'Advanced Options', and tweak as you see fit.

5. **Who Can Access?** This is where you curate your audience. Whether you want all users of your Mac (On left, choose Users & Groups > Choose name(s) > press Select) or specific friends and family from your network (Choose Network Users or Network Groups > Choose name(s) > Select), you decide. You can even select someone from your contacts, creating a special sharing-only account for them (choose Contacts to the left > choose name > Select > create password > press Create Account).

6. **Defining Access Levels**: Just like you would not give everyone the key to your home, you might want to define how much access someone has to your files. Choices range from full 'Read & Write', 'Read Only,' 'Write Only' access to the more restrictive 'No Access'.

7. **Press Done**

8. **Advanced Options for the Tech-Savvy**

While many might be content with the basic sharing options, some might wish to dive a bit deeper. Advanced options let you:

- Allow guest users for temporary access.

- Ensure encrypted connections for added security.

- Share as a Time Machine backup destination for safeguarding memories.

To access these, just control-click the shared folder's name and opt for 'Advanced Options'.

13.1 Sharing via chat apps on your Mac!

1. The Digital Coffee Table Gathering: Chat Apps

Think of chat apps as your digital coffee table – a space where friends and family gather around, except this table stretches across continents! First, you will need a chat app. MacOS Ventura supports several, but for this guide, let us focus on the most user-friendly and widely used: iMessage (already pre-installed on your Mac).

2. Setting the Stage: Opening iMessage

- Find the blue speech bubble icon (that's iMessage) on your Mac's dock or in the Applications folder.

- Open the app. If it is your first time, you will be prompted to log in with your Apple ID.

3. Starting a Conversation or Continuing One

- On the top-left corner, click the pen and paper icon to start a new conversation.

- Alternatively, click on an existing conversation from the left sidebar.

4. Sharing the Treasures: Attachments and Content

Sharing in iMessage is as easy as drag and drop:

- **Photos & Videos**: Have a beautiful photo from the last family gathering or a video of your grandchild's first steps? Drag the file from your desktop (or any folder) and drop it into the conversation window.

- **Documents & Files**: It is a recipe you want to share or an article you found interesting. The drag and drop method work here too!

- **Location & Links**: Planning a meet-up or finding an interesting online read? Click the 'A' icon above the typing space, where you will find options to share your location or any link.

5. Voice Notes for That Personal Touch

Sometimes, texts do not do justice. For those moments:

- Click on the microphone icon beside the text box.

- Record your heartfelt message, be it a birthday wish, a lullaby, or just a simple 'I miss you.'

- Once done, release to send. Yes, it is that simple!

6. Emojis, Stickers, and Animojis: Add a Pinch of Fun

Gone are the days when chats were plain text. Add flavor to your messages:

- Click on the smiling emoji icon in the text box.

- Explore and insert fun emojis, stickers, or even Animojis (animated characters that mirror your facial expressions).

7. Engage in Group Conversations

Family group chats can be a whirlwind of joy, updates, and occasional banters:

- Start a new message.

- Add multiple contacts.

- Now everyone can join in the fun, sharing photos, stories, and memorable moments.

13.2 Email Sharing

1. The Virtual Pigeon: Understanding Email

In the days of yore, pigeons delivered messages. In the digital realm, consider email as your swift and dependable pigeon, just without the feathers.

2. Setting Sail: Accessing the Mail App

- The Mail app on MacOS Ventura boasts a postage stamp icon. Find it on your dock or launch it from the Applications folder.

- If it is your first time, you will be prompted to sign in. Enter your email credentials, and let the journey begin!

3. Writing a New Tale: Composing an Email

- Within Mail, spot the button labeled "New" or the pen icon to begin crafting your message.

- Enter the recipient's email in the "To:" field. Think of this as charting the coordinates for our pigeon's journey.

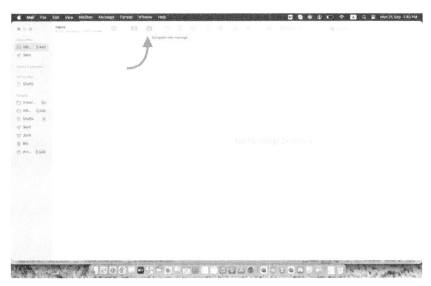

4. Sharing Your Treasures: Attaching Files

Ah, the heart of our adventure!

- **Drag and Drop**: From your desktop or any folder, drag the item you wish to share and drop it into the body of your email.

- **Paperclip Icon**: Click on the little paperclip (or sometimes a camera icon for photos) to navigate to your file and select it.

5. The Magical Quill: Writing Your Message

- Beneath the subject line, you will find a vast white expanse, waiting for your words. Share your stories, thoughts, or even a simple greeting.

- Not fond of typing? Use the built-in Dictation feature. Simply press the "Function) key twice, speak your message, and watch as your words magically appear!

6. Embellishing Your Message: Formatting and Fun

Why send plain scrolls when you can add a splash of color?

- Highlight your text and choose the "A" icon to reveal a world of fonts, sizes, and colors.

- Add emojis by pressing "Ctrl + Cmd + Space" simultaneously. From smiley faces to tiny digital pigeons, express yourself!

7. Setting Sail: Sending Your Message

Once your treasures are aboard, and your message is penned, click the "Send" button, usually depicted by a paper plane. Your virtual pigeon is now en route!

8. When Adventure Calls: Accessing Received Emails

- On the left pane, click "Inbox". Here lie messages from fellow adventurers, waiting to be discovered.

- Double-click on an email to delve into its contents. Attachments are usually represented by paperclip icons.

13.3 Social Media Sharing

1. Deciphering the Digital Map: What is social media?

In the vast digital ocean, social media platforms are bustling islands, where people gather to share stories, photographs, and snippets of their lives. Consider them modern-day town squares, where one can showcase their latest adventures, creations, or thoughts.

2. Launching the Expedition: Accessing social media

Most social media platforms have dedicated applications available on the Mac App Store. You can also access them through Safari, MacOS Ventura's trusted compass or web browser.

3. Crafting Your Digital Scroll: Posting on social media

Each platform offers a unique way to weave your tale:

- **Facebook**: Seek the 'What's on your mind?' box. Here, you can pen your thoughts, add photos, videos, or even create an album of a recent voyage or family gathering.

- **Twitter (renamed X)**: Within the 280-character limit, send out 'tweets' - quick messages or reflections. Attach photos or videos to make your story vibrant.

- **Instagram**: Tailored for photographs, use the '+' icon to add a snapshot of a moment. Add a caption and hashtag or two like #VenturaAdventures.

4. Sharing Treasures: Uploading Photos and Videos

Across platforms, there is a universal symbol for adding media – a camera or a gallery icon. Clicking on it allows you to:

- Choose photos/videos from your Mac's library.

- Add filters or edit them to add a touch of magic.

5. To Tag or Not to Tag: Engaging with Fellow Explorers

To mention a fellow adventurer in your posts:

- **Facebook & Instagram**: Use '@' followed by their name. E.g., **@CaptainHawkins**.

- **Twitter**: The same '@' symbol followed by their handle. E.g., **@GoldenAgeExplorer**.

Tagging pulls them into your digital narrative, making moments more memorable.

6. Setting Your Privacy Compass

Every island in the digital ocean has its privacy settings:

- Customize who can view your posts - be it the entire world, just your friends, or a select crew.

- Adjust settings in the privacy or account section of each platform.

7. Engaging in the Digital Festivities: Liking, Commenting, and Sharing

Interaction is the heart of social media:

- **Like**: A straightforward way to show appreciation. Usually symbolized by a thumbs-up, heart, or star.

- **Comment**: Share your thoughts or compliments. Find the speech bubble or comment box.

- **Share/Retweet**: Share another's story on your timeline, spreading the tale to your crew.

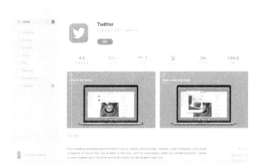 

14   How to do the backup and use iCloud

Ahoy, fearless digital explorers of MacOS Ventura! While we have sailed through many digital landscapes, it is time we check on safeguarding your treasures. In the olden days, pirates buried their gold; in the digital age, we back up our data. And fear not, for this does not involve shovels or maps marked with an 'X'. Let the clouds (iClouds, to be precise) carry your riches safely.

1. The Cloud's Silver Lining: What's iCloud?

Imagine a magical chest in the sky, holding all your precious memories, documents, and data. That is iCloud! It is Apple's online storage service, keeping your treasures safe and accessible anytime, anywhere.

2. Setting Sail: Setting up iCloud

- Navigate to **Apple menu > System Preferences**.

- Click on **Apple ID**.

- If you are not signed in, enter your Apple ID and password.

- In the sidebar, select **iCloud** and check the box next to it.

3. Storing Your Booty: Choosing What to Store on iCloud

Once you are in iCloud preferences:

- You will spot a list of apps using iCloud. Check boxes next to apps like Photos, Mail, Contacts, and others you want to store in the cloud.

- The bar at the bottom showcases how much storage you have used and have available.

- Want all your iCloud Drive contents on your Mac and included in your Time Machine backup? Simply head to **System Settings** > **Apple ID** > **iCloud** and uncheck the box for **Optimize Mac Storage**.

- **iCloud Photos:** To ensure all your precious memories are safely stored in full resolution on your Mac, go to **Photos** > **Settings** > **iCloud** and choose **"Download Originals to this Mac."**

4. Time Machine: Traveling Back to Safeguard

Apart from iCloud, MacOS Ventura has a built-in backup solution, aptly named Time Machine, letting you sail back in time to recover lost data.

- Connect an external hard drive or a supported network volume to your Mac.

- Setting up - System Settings > General > Time Machine > Add Backup Disk

- Go to **Apple menu** > **System Preferences** > **Time Machine**.

- Click **Select Backup Disk** and choose your external drive.

- Check the box **"Back Up Automatically"** to let Time Machine regularly back up your Mac.

5. Exploring iCloud.com: Access from Any Shore

You do not need to be on your ship (read: Mac) to access your treasures!

- Simply navigate to iCloud.com on any device.

- Enter your Apple ID and password.

- Voila! Your documents, photos, and more are accessible from any port.

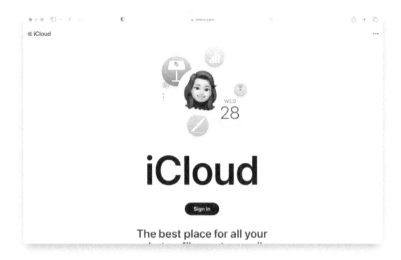

6. Increasing Your Treasure Chest: Upgrading iCloud Storage

The basic iCloud comes with 5GB for free. But for those with grander adventures:

- Navigate to **Apple menu** > **System Preferences** > **Apple ID** > **iCloud**.

- Click **Manage** at the bottom right.

- Click **Change Storage Plan** or **Buy More Storage** and select a plan that suits your treasure-holding needs

7. Safeguarding the Skies: Security and iCloud

With treasures come pirates. Ensure the safety of your digital booty:

- Activate **two-factor authentication** for your Apple ID.

- Regularly update your password and keep it complex.

- Keep your Mac's software updated for the latest security enhancements.

Navigating the Time Machine Timeline

Lost a file? Time Machine is your compass. Click on the Time Machine icon in your menu bar and choose **"Browse Time Machine backups."** Then, just like choosing a destination on a map, select the items you want to restore.

And if disaster strikes – say, a damaged operating system or startup disk – reinstall macOS on your Mac. Afterward, the Time Machine will guide you back to your treasures.

Anchoring with a Fresh Start: Reinstalling macOS

Sometimes, the best way to move forward is to start fresh. If you ever find your MacOS in choppy waters, you can reinstall it. Post-installation, the Time Machine is ready with a lifeboat to bring back all your personal files.

For the more tech-savvy sailors who like being prepared, creating a bootable installer for macOS is like having an extra compass onboard. This ensures you are never lost, no matter how stormy the digital seas get.

A Clean Slate: Restoring Factory Settings

Starting afresh can be liberating. Erase your Mac and let macOS Recovery breathe new life into it with a fresh macOS installation.

15 Widgets

Imagine a world where tiny virtual assistants sit right on your desktop, always ready to give you a snapshot of valuable information or tools without you having to delve deep into applications. This world exists, and in the realm of macOS Ventura, these assistants are called "Widgets."

A Tale of Digital Elves: What are Widgets?

In the heart of macOS Ventura, there are countless digital elves—**Widgets**—waiting to make your life simpler. Imagine them as little windows into your favorite apps, giving you a glimpse of the essentials without opening the full program. Designed to present a chunk of useful information or a handy tool, Widgets light up your Mac's desktop and make your digital journey smoother and more delightful.

They display live, frequently updated information. Checking the forecast, peeping into your to-do list, tracking your system's health, or even changing the tune you are listening to, can all be achieved swiftly with widgets.

For example, if in the real world you had a tiny weather fairy sitting on your desk, telling you whether to take an umbrella today, wouldn't that be helpful? In the world of macOS Ventura, this fairy exists as a Weather Widget, constantly updating and ensuring you are prepared for Mother Nature's moods.

Why Widgets?

1. **Instant Glance**: Instead of launching an entire app to check your stock, weather, or calendar events, Widgets give you a quick preview.

2. **Space Savers**: Unlike the traditional application window, Widgets are compact. They are like the magical pocket watch of the digital world, small but enormous in utility.

3. **Customization**: Widgets are not one-size-fits-all. They can be resized and rearranged, allowing you to curate your digital workspace as you see fit.

Types of Widgets: The Many Elves of macOS Ventura

- **Mini Elves (Small Widgets)**: Perfect for a quick glance, like the current date or your next calendar event.

- **Medium Elves (Medium Widgets)**: A bit more detail here—like a summarized view of your week's calendar or the current playback song.

- **Giant Elves (Large Widgets)**: For when you want the bigger picture. A detailed weather forecast or a month's view of your calendar.

How to Add Widgets

1. **Gateway to Widgets**: Click in the top right corner of your screen. This opens the Notification Center.

2. **Explorer Mode**: Scroll to the bottom and find the 'Edit Widgets' button. Clicking it will reveal a plethora of available widgets.

3. **Choosing Your Companions**: Spot a widget you like? Click on the '+' icon beside it to add. Some widgets offer varied sizes. Click on a size to preview it.

Customizing Widgets

- Right-click (or Control-click) on a Widget.

- Choose 'Edit Widget' from the dropdown.

- Tweak and adjust as you see fit. Each Widget offers its own set of customizations.

Managing Widgets

Just as a wizard control where their spells fly, you can control where your widgets reside:

1. **Relocation**: Widgets can be dragged to your preferred location.

2. **Dismissing the Magic**: If you ever feel the need to send a widget back to the virtual ether, just click on the '-' icon.

Top Widgets for macOS

- **Weather**: Always be prepared, come rain or shine.

- **Calendar**: Keep tabs on your appointments and special dates.

- **Calculator**: Quick sums, no full app needed.

- **Battery**: Stay informed about your MacBook's energy levels.

- **Music**: Control tunes from your desktop.

- **SideNotes**: Keep important notes readily accessible.

- **Moment**: Countdown to momentous events, ensuring you never miss out.

How to Use Widgets on macOS Ventura

Add Widgets to Notification Center

The steps:

1. Launch the **Notification Center application** on your Mac.

2. Click the **Edit Widgets button** located at the bottom of the Notification Center.

3. Look for the widget you want to see in the list of widget categories, and then either search for it or click on the category you want, such as **"Clock."** There are many sizes available for some widgets; selecting one allows you to get a preview of the information it displays.

4. Position the cursor over the widget in the preview, then click the **Add button** to add it to the list of active widgets you currently have available.

5. Simply dragging the new widget higher or lower in the list of active widgets will allow you to reorganize its position in the set. Click the **Remove button** located on the new widget if you have concluded that you do not want it.

6. When you are through adding widgets, click the **Done button** that is located at the bottom of the widgets that are now active.

Customize Widgets in Notification Center

The steps:

1. Launch the **Notification Center application** on your Mac.

2. Click the **Edit Widgets button** located at the bottom of the Notification Center.

3. In your collection of currently running widgets, do any one of the following actions:

Modify the information shown by a widget: To choose a widget, move the cursor over it. If the words **Edit Widget** show underneath the widget's name, it means that you can modify the information. Click the widget to toggle it. Alter the settings by clicking the highlighted information or selecting other alternatives. To choose a different list of reminders, for instance, you can use the List widget for Reminders by clicking the list that is highlighted. When you are done, you may exit the widget by clicking the Done button.

To adjust the size of a widget, do the following: Control-click a widget, and then choose a smaller size from the drop-down menu that appears.

4. When you are through making changes to the widgets, click the **Done button** that is located at the bottom of the active widgets.

Remove Widgets from Notification Center

If you do no longer want widgets to appear in the notification center, you can remove them by following the steps below:

1. Launch the **Notification Center app** on your Mac.

While holding down the **Option key**, drag the cursor over the widget you want to delete, and then click the **Delete button** when you are through.

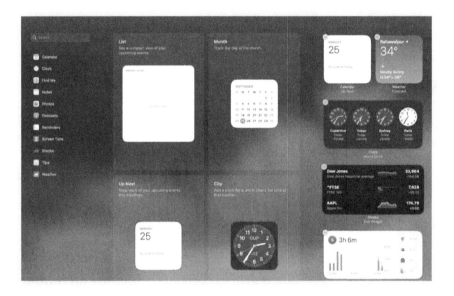

The Magic of Widgets

Venturing into the world of macOS Ventura might seem like diving into a new realm, but with your army of Widget elves by your side, every task becomes simpler. Embrace these mini helpers, customize them to your heart content, and let the magic of macOS Ventura enhance your digital experience.

16 How to connect the iPhone to your laptop

16.1 How to Sync your iPhone & iPad with Your Mac on Ventura OS

You can choose which data to synchronize between your Mac and the device. You can synchronize every item of a certain kind (for example, all your movies or photos). Alternatively, you can choose certain things, which provide you with greater control (for instance, some of your movies and some of your books).

- When you synchronize your device and Mac, the items are updated once you choose the material you wish to synchronize.
- You must use a USB or USB-C connection to connect your device to your Mac to set up syncing for the first time. The device symbol appears in the Finder sidebar once you connect it, and choosing the icon shows synchronization choices. Next, you decide which things to synchronize.

Sync music to your device

1. Connect your device to your Mac. Your device can be connected through Wi-Fi, a USB or USB-C cable, or both.

2. Choose the device from the Finder sidebar in your Mac's Finder.

3. In the button bar, choose **Music**.

4. To enable music synchronization, check the **"Sync music onto [device name]"** box.

5. By checking the option, synchronization is configured to download all your music to your device.

6. Select **"Selected playlist, artists, albums, and genres"** to synchronize a certain group of songs.

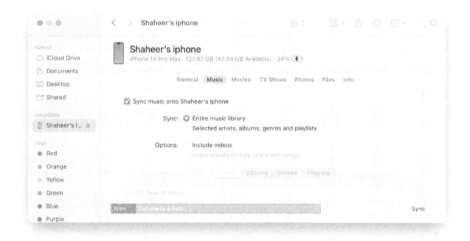

7. Check the box next to each song in the music list you wish to synchronize. For each item you do not want to synchronize, deselect the checkbox. For a list of your material categorized by artists, albums, genres, or playlists, choose the appropriate link.

8. Pick synchronization options:

   - To add videos during synchronizing, check the **"Include videos"** box.
   - To include voice memos while synchronizing, check the **"Include voice memos"** box.
   - To have your Mac automatically fill the space on your device with music while synchronizing, check the **"Automatically fill free space with songs"** checkbox. If you do not have enough space to synchronize your whole music collection to your device but have a large music library, choose this option.

9. Click **Apply** when you are ready to synchronize.

You can decide to automatically synchronize your Mac and your device every time you connect them. Click the **Eject button** ⏏ in the Finder sidebar before removing your device from your Mac.

Sync Movies to your Device

The steps:

1. Connect your iPhone/iPad to your Mac. Your device can be connected through Wi-Fi, a USB or USB-C cable, or both.

2. Choose the device from the Finder sidebar in your Mac's Finder. Check if your device does not display in the sidebar if you connect your device to your Mac using a USB connection.

3. Select **Movies** from the menu bar.

4. To enable film synchronization, choose the **"Sync films onto [device name]"** checkbox. By checking the option, synchronization is configured to download all your movies to your device.

5. Pick the **"Automatically include"** checkbox, then select the number of recently viewed or unwatched movies from the menu to synchronize a selection of movies.

6. Tick the boxes next to each movie in the film list that you wish to synchronize. Uncheck the box next to any movie you do not wish to synchronize.

7. Click **Apply** when you are ready to synchronize.

You can decide to automatically synchronize your Mac and your device every time you connect them. Click the **Eject button** ⏏ in the Finder sidebar before removing your device from your Mac.

Remove Automatically Synced Movies from your Device

Delete the undesired movie from your Mac, then synchronize your device to remove it from both your Mac and device. These procedures should be followed if you want to save the movie on your Mac but just delete it from your device:

1. Connect your device to your Mac. Your device can be connected through Wi-Fi, a USB or USB-C cable, or both.

2. In the Finder on your Mac, click **Movies** in the button bar after choosing your device from the sidebar.

3. Deselect the checkbox next to the movie you want to delete from the list of the films.

4. Then synchronize your Mac with the device.

16.2 Transform Your iPhone Into a Webcam on Your Mac

Imagine turning your iPhone – with its stellar camera – into a webcam for your Mac. Sounds incredible, right? macOS Ventura and iOS 16 make this a reality, introducing a seamless integration called **Continuity Camera**. Dive into this modern wizardry with us, step by step.

The Initial Preparations

Before casting the spell, ensure everything is in order:

1. **Updates**: Make certain your Mac runs macOS Ventura, while your iPhone should dance with iOS 16.

2. **Unified Identity**: A shared Apple ID should identify both devices.

3. **Communication**: Both gadgets should have Wi-Fi and Bluetooth toggled on.

4. **Compatibility**: Not all machines possess this magic. Visit Apple's official page for "Continuity" system requirements to check compatibility.

5. **Mounting**: For a stable view, mount your iPhone. Apple provides more about this in their Continuity Camera article.

Wield Your iPhone as a Webcam

1. **Begin the Ritual**: On your Mac, open camera-enabled apps, say, FaceTime or Photo Booth.

2. **Selection**: Navigate to the app's settings or menu bar, choosing your iPhone for camera or microphone duties.

3. **Action**: Your iPhone, now a trusted sidekick, starts capturing audio or video with its rear camera prowess.

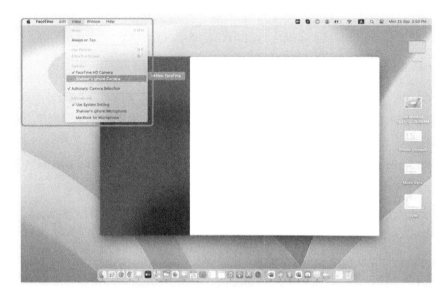

Note: If you are using the iPhone solely as a microphone for a camera-less Mac, ensure the iPhone is in landscape mode, locked, and still.

Controls at your Fingertips:

- **Pause**: Tap 'Pause' on your iPhone or unlock it.

- **Resume**: Tap 'Resume' or lock the iPhone.

- **Discontinue**: Simply quit the app on your Mac.

- **Disconnect**: On your iPhone, select 'Disconnect' to remove it from the camera and microphone lists.

- **Reconnection**: Reconnect with a USB cord if you wish to reintroduce your iPhone.

Charging Tip: If your iPhone yearns for some juice while this feature is active, connect using a USB cable for optimal results.

Automation & Preference Magic

Your Mac can auto select your iPhone for certain apps. For this sorcery to work, ensure the iPhone is near, screen-locked, in landscape orientation, and stationary. Also, the camera should face you, unobscured. If previously used as a webcam, some apps might remember your iPhone as the default.

Amplifying Audio through iPhone

Make your iPhone the prime microphone for your Mac. Visit **Apple menu > System Settings**, then select **Sound**. In the audio device list, choose your iPhone. Continuity magic will initiate, capturing audio through your iPhone.

Visual Enhancements

When your iPhone assumes the role of a webcam, the Control Center lets you weave in visual magic. You can light up your workspace or make yourself the star with Desk View and Studio Light, respectively.

Troubleshooting Tips

If you are fumbling to see your iPhone as an option:

1. Connect via USB and reassess.

2. Ensure:

- Your iPhone model is an iPhone XR or its successors.

- Both devices are updated with the latest OS versions.

- Your iPhone has the Continuity Camera enabled (Settings > General > AirPlay & Handoff).

- Trust is established between your iPhone and Mac.

- Wi-Fi, Bluetooth, and two-factor authentication are active on both devices.

- Both devices are identified by a shared Apple ID.

- Proximity: Keep devices within thirty feet.

- No internet sharing is occurring.

- The app you are using is up to date.

In this digital era, combining the strengths of two Apple devices enhances user experience exponentially. Your Mac and iPhone, when combined, can create an unparalleled virtual interaction, proving once again that sometimes, two are indeed better than one!

16.3 Bridging Mac to Windows: A Seamless Connection

Imagine a world where your Mac, with all its sleekness, communicates smoothly with a Windows computer. Sounds like tech harmony, doesn't it? With macOS Ventura, this dream becomes reality. Let us journey together into the realms of Mac-to-Windows connectivity.

Setting The Stage

Before your Mac and Windows computer can chat, the Windows PC must be ready to mingle.

- **Preparation**: First, set up your windows computer to be open for sharing with Mac users. If you are unfamiliar with this process, our chapter on 'Setting up Windows for Mac Users' can guide you.

Connect Through Browsing

1. **Summoning The Portal**: On your Mac, head to Finder, select Go > Connect to Server, and then click 'Browse'.

2. **Finding the Companion**: Spot the Windows computer you wish to connect to and double-click its icon.

3. **Credentials & Access**: Should a prompt appear, click 'Connect As'. At times, the network or workgroup details might be necessary. If lost, contact your Windows PC's owner or network admin.

4. **Remembering Your Voyage**: To bypass the hassle of repetitive logins, select "Remember this password in my keychain."

Direct Address Entry

1. **The Direct Approach**: On your Mac, within Finder, go to Go > Connect to Server.

2. **Specifics**: Input the network address of the windows computer, typically following this format: **smb://IPaddress/sharename** or **smb://DNSname/sharename**.

3. **Gateways & Credentials**: Upon entering the address, a screen may guide you to type a workgroup name and associated credentials.

4. **Recalling Past Journeys**: To remember your credentials for future connections, opt for "Remember this password in my keychain".

   The Physical Bridge: Ethernet Cable

1. **Joining Forces**: An Ethernet cable is the bond. Connect your Mac and Windows PC. If your Mac lacks an Ethernet port, use a USB-to-Ethernet converter.

2. **Inception of A Mini-Network**: This connection spawns a miniature network exclusive to your computers

3. **Windows' Open Arms**: Ensure the Windows computer's file sharing is active. If unfamiliar, consult the computer's manual.

4. **Firewall Passage**: Disable the Internet Connection Firewall on Windows or open TCP port 445.

5. **Commencement**: Back on your Mac, opt for Go > Connect to Server, then either click 'Browse' or key in the network address.

Retracing Steps to Past Connections

Sometimes, familiar roads are the easiest to tread:

1. **Recent Journeys**: On your Mac, under the Apple menu, navigate to Recent Items, choosing from the list of known servers.

2. **Favorites**: Mark a shared computer or server as a favorite. This makes future connections just a click away!

Troubles on the Horizon?

If the shared computer seems elusive or remains disconnected, it might be unavailable, or you lack access permissions. It is time to engage with the guardian of that computer – its owner, or the network administrator.

16.4 How to transfer music from PC

Music has always been an essential part of our lives, representing both the era we grew up in and the moments we cherish. As you move to macOS Ventura, why leave your treasured melodies behind? Let us embark on a melodious journey from your PC to your Mac.

Setting the Rhythm

Before the grand musical procession begins, let us prepare your Mac's stage to welcome the tuneful arrivals.

iCloud Harmony: Streaming the Clouds

1. **Accessing iCloud**: On your PC, log in to iCloud.com.

2. **Into the Cloud**: Upload your tracks to iCloud Music Library.

3. **From the Clouds to Mac**: On your Mac, sign in with the same Apple ID and let the music rain down from iCloud.

Apple Music or iTunes: The Orchestra Leaders

If you are an Apple Music subscriber or have a penchant for iTunes:

1. **iTunes Ensemble**: Install iTunes on your PC, if you have not already.

2. **Gathering the Tunes**: In iTunes, gather your melodies by adding them to your Library.

3. **Homeward Bound**: Use the 'Home Sharing' feature in iTunes to seamlessly import the tracks to your Mac.

Music app's Grand Overture

The Music app, your personal maestro in macOS Ventura, makes importing your tunes a lyrical ballet.

- **Step 1:** Open the **Music app** on your Mac, the stage where all your melodies will be performed.

- **Step 2:** At the top menu, click on **File**. Depending on your prior settings, you will see either **Add to Library** or **Import**.

If you are wondering about the distinction: If you have chosen the option "Copy files to Music Media folder when adding to library" under the Files settings, the Music app will display **Import** instead of **Add to Library**.

- **Step 3:** A dialog box appears, guiding you to your files. Navigate through this, find the songs or music videos on your PC you wish to transfer, then click **Open**.

- **Step 4:** If you are importing an entire folder, rest assured that every musical note, every file within, will be integrated into your Music app's collection.

The Encore: Drag and Drop Serenade

If you fancy a quicker, more intuitive approach:

- Simply open the location of your music files or folders on your Mac.

- Drag your chosen pieces and drop them into the Music app's window. Witness the seamless dance as they find their place in your library.

Manual Migration: The Classic Vinyl Way

For those who appreciate the age-old art of manual transfer:

1. **External Symphony**: Utilize an external drive or USB stick. Copy music from your PC and paste it into the drive.

2. **Eject and Connect**: Safely eject the drive from the PC and connect it to your Mac.

3. **Final Act**: Transfer your melodies from the external drive to your Mac's Music folder or directly into the Music app.

The Digital Maestros: Third-party Apps

Some digital conductors can make the music march coordinated between different platforms:

1. **Select a Maestro**: Apps like 'AnyTrans' or 'Dr. Fone - Phone Manager' can be your maestros.

2. **Synchronized Beats**: Follow the app's instructions to synchronize music from your PC to Mac effortlessly.

17   Most common and life saver tips and tricks

macOS is a powerhouse operating system that keeps getting better every year. Yet, many of its features remain underutilized or unknown by a large number of its users. Whether you are new to macOS or have been using it for years, there are always ways to work more efficiently, save time, or simply get more out of your device.

macOS Ventura, the latest iteration, comes with numerous tips and tricks that can drastically enhance your user experience, especially for seniors. Here is a list of some indispensable features:

Unlock your Mac with an Apple Watch:

A seamless integration of Apple's ecosystem lets you unlock your Mac instantly using your Apple Watch. This saves you the hassle of typing in your password or using Touch ID every time.

Spotlight Search for Swift Calculations:

Need to do some quick math? Instead of opening the Calculator app, use Spotlight Search. Just press Command + Space and type in your equation to get results instantly.

Efficiently Use Split Screen:

Work on two apps side-by-side without the need to switch between them continuously. Simply hover over the green circle in the top left corner of a window to use this feature.

Organize with Multiple Desktops:

Separate your work from leisure or manage multiple projects efficiently by using several desktops. Access this feature through Mission Control.

Hot Corners - Your Quick Actions:

Want a quick way to access certain features? Set up Hot Corners to perform specific actions just by moving your cursor to any of the four screen corners.

Transform your Mac into an AirPlay Receiver:

Mirroring your iPhone or iPad to your Mac becomes a breeze with the AirPlay receiver feature.

Bulk Rename Files:

If you have ever had a batch of files that needed renaming, macOS has you covered. Select them all, right-click, and rename them in bulk to save time.

Minimalist Desktop with Auto-hide Features:

Hide the Dock or Menu Bar for a cleaner workspace. They will pop back up when you move your cursor to their locations.

Access Saved Wi-Fi Passwords:

No more forgotten Wi-Fi passwords. Retrieve them from the Keychain Access app with ease.

Dynamic Wallpapers - Fresh Every Time:

Your desktop wallpaper evolves throughout the day with dynamic wallpaper, adjusting to your local time.

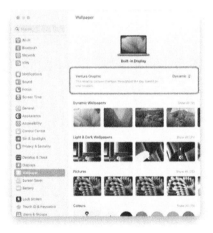

Use Dictation for Hands-free Typing:

Speak, and macOS will type it out for you. Perfect for those moments when you are multitasking.

A Complete Overview with Mission Control:

View all your open applications and windows with a simple gesture or button press.

Quickly Switch Between Apps:

Use the Command + Tab shortcut to cycle through your open apps quickly.

Force Quit Unresponsive Apps:

If an app is freezing up, use Command + Q to force quit and get back to work.

Instant File Deletion:

Bypass the Trash and delete files instantly by holding the Command and Option keys, then pressing Delete.

Easy Screenshots:

Grab a quick screenshot with Command + Shift + 3 or access the dedicated Screenshot app for more options.

Define Words with Ease:

Get definitions instantly either by right-clicking and selecting "Look Up" or by force touching on a trackpad.

Swift Notification Center Access:

Access your notifications with a simple swipe, keeping you updated without the hassle.

Focus Mode for Distraction-free Work:

Turn on Focus mode to minimize disruptions and prioritize your work notifications.

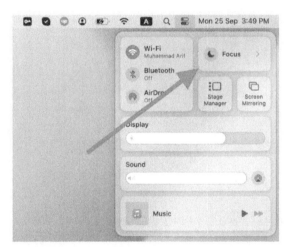

Efficient Image Conversion:

Convert images to different formats or sizes directly from the Finder.

Customize App and Folder Icons:

Give your macOS a personalized touch by changing icons to suit your preferences.

Live Text from Photos:

Select, copy, or look up text from photos using the Live Text feature.

Maximize Battery Life:

The latest macOS provides improved settings and features to ensure your device runs efficiently, helping you get the most out of your battery.

Create File Templates with Stationery Pad:

- Use the Stationery Pad feature in Finder to automatically open a copy of any file. This ensures the original remains unedited.

- Perfect for document templates like Photoshop designs, HTML/CSS skeletons, or Word document invoicing.

- Activate by right-clicking the desired file -> Get Info -> check Stationery Pad. The next time you open this file, a fresh copy is created automatically.

Unveil Hidden Preview Formats:

- In Preview, Option-click the Format dropdown to reveal additional file-saving options.

Never Lose Your Way in Safari with SnapBack:

- Easily return to your original search results in Safari, no matter how many links you have clicked on.

- Access SnapBack via History -> Search Results SnapBack or use the shortcut Command-Option-S.

Smart Control with Hot Corners:

- Assign specific actions to screen corners (like accessing Notification Center or Mission Control).

- Prevent accidental triggers by using modifier keys. Set this up in System Settings -> Desktop & Dock -> Hot Corners. Choose a corner and assign a function using a modifier key (e.g., Shift-Command).

Enhance Your Dock with More Recent Apps:

- Display more than the default three recently used apps in the Dock.

- Customize the number using Terminal commands. For instance, showing ten recent apps involves the command: **defaults write com. apple. dock show-recent-count -int ten; killall Dock**.

Symmetrical Window Resizing:

- Hold the Option key while dragging a window corner to resize it symmetrically from its center point.

Special Alerts for VIP Emails:

- In Apple Mail, set distinct notifications for emails from your VIPs.

- Create a custom rule in Mail Settings to play specific sounds or bounce the Dock icon for VIP emails.

Keep Notes on Top of Other Windows:

- In the Notes app, float a note over other app windows so it stays visible.

- Open a note in a new window and select Window -> Keep on Top from the menu bar.

Personalize Finder's Toolbar:

- Drag and drop apps, files, or folders onto the Finder's toolbar for easy access. Ensure you hold the Command (⌘) key while doing so.

Instant Access to Specific System Settings:

- Use the Option key plus a function key to open associated System Settings. E.g., Option-F11/12 takes you directly to the Sound pane.

Use Split Screen for Multitasking Working with multiple applications? macOS makes it simple to view two apps side by side without having to manually resize windows. With one app active, click and hold the green maximize button on the top left of the window. Drag the window to the left or right side of the screen, then choose the other app you wish to view on the opposite side. Now you have a split screen!

Dictation for Hands-free Writing macOS comes with a powerful dictation feature, which is great for hands-free writing. Navigate to System Settings -> Keyboard -> Dictation, then turn on Dictation. Whenever you want to dictate instead of type, press the "Fn" (Function) key twice and start speaking.

Instant Dictionary Definitions Reading or writing and stumbled upon a word you are not familiar with? Hover over the word and tap with three fingers on your trackpad. This will instantly pop up a dictionary definition of the word.

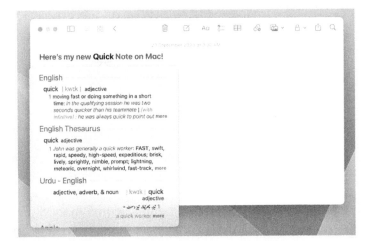

Sign Documents with Preview No need to print, sign, and scan documents. Open the PDF in Preview, click on the Markup Toolbar (a toolbox icon), then select the Signature option to sign using your trackpad or capture a written signature using your Mac's camera.

Organize your Desktop with Stacks Keep your desktop clutter-free with Stacks. Right-click on your desktop and select "Use Stacks". macOS will automatically group files by type, ensuring your desktop remains tidy.

Quick Emoji Access While typing, press Control + Command + Space to bring up an emoji picker. This will allow you to easily insert your favorite emojis without breaking your flow.

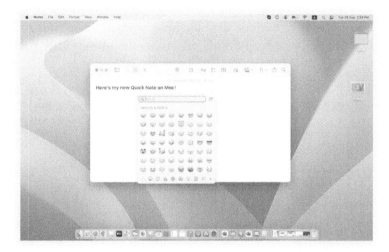

Group FaceTime Calls You're not limited to one-on-one chats with FaceTime. Start a group FaceTime call by adding more contacts before initiating the call or during an ongoing one.

Create Custom Keyboard Shortcuts If there is a specific menu option in an app you use frequently, go to System Settings -> Keyboard -> Shortcuts -> App Shortcuts and add a custom shortcut for it.

Use Picture-in-Picture Mode While watching a video in Safari, right-click on the video player and select "Enter Picture-in-Picture". This will allow the video to play in a small, movable window while you work on other things.

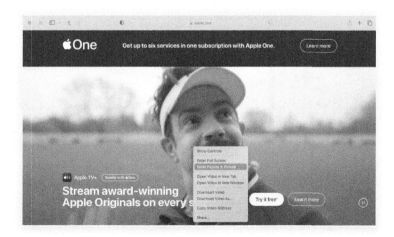

Scan Documents with your iPhone If you have an iPhone, you can quickly scan documents directly into your Mac without needing a scanner. Right-click in Finder or on your Desktop, hover over "Import from iPhone or iPad", and choose "Scan Documents". Use your iPhone to take a scan, and it will instantly appear on your Mac.

Shift to Night Shift Mode Working late? Reduce the blue light emitted from your screen by turning on Night Shift. Go to System Settings -> Displays -> Night Shift, and schedule or manually adjust the color temperature for your screen.

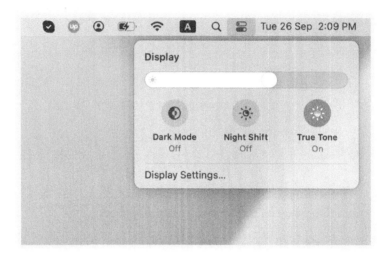

Quick Access to Wi-Fi Passwords If you have previously connected to a Wi-Fi network on your Mac or iPhone, the password is saved in your Keychain. To retrieve it, open Keychain Access, find the Wi-Fi network name, double-click on it, and check "Show Password" to reveal it.

Silent Clicking on the Trackpad If you prefer a quieter experience when using your MacBook, navigate to System Settings -> Trackpad -> Silent Clicking to mute the click sound.

Spotlight as a Calculator Instead of opening the Calculator app, you can use Spotlight to do quick calculations. Simply press Command + Space to open Spotlight, type in your math problem, and see the results in real-time.

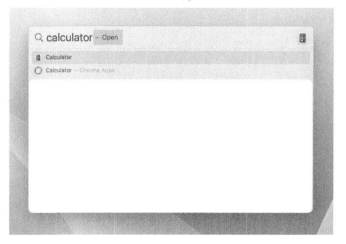

Hide and Show the Dock Instantly For more screen space, instantly hide the Dock by pressing Command + Option + D. Press the same combination to bring it back.

18 FAQs

When was the release of macOS 13 Ventura?

On October 24, 2022.

How is macOS Ventura different from previous versions?

macOS Ventura boasts a range of updates including refined visuals, improved accessibility features, enhanced privacy settings, and tighter integration with Apple's ecosystem.

How much does it cost to get macOS 13 Ventura?

It is free (in the sense that it may be downloaded for free from the internet), and the entire size of the download will be around 12.5 GB.

What is macOS Ventura?

macOS Ventura is Apple's newest operating system for Mac computers. Think of it as the brain behind your Mac, dictating how your computer looks, feels, and operates. It is the successor to macOS Big Sur and brings forth a suite of new features, enhancements, and security upgrades.

Is my older Mac compatible with Ventura?

Apple is known for its inclusivity, and most Macs from 2015 onwards can run Ventura. However, it is always good to check through Chapter 2 of this book for a comprehensive list of compatible devices.

Does macOS Ventura support all programs that need 64-bit processing?

ANS. No, the 64-bit program requires that all the components and resources that it uses also be 64-bit (compatible). Apple has confirmed that some features will be incompatible with macOS versions 10.15 and later.

How Do I Install/Update to macOS Ventura?

- Launch the App Store and search for "macOS Ventura."

- Click "Download" and follow the on-screen prompts. Restart when prompted and let your Mac do the magic.

How Can I Customize My Desktop?

- Right-click on your desktop, choose "Change Desktop Background" for wallpaper options.

- For icon organization, drag and drop them as desired.

- To adjust your Dock, head to System Preferences > Dock & Menu Bar.

I am not tech-savvy. Is it hard to upgrade to Ventura?

Absolutely not! Apple ensures that upgrading is a straightforward process. Open the App Store, find macOS Ventura, and click "Download." Follow the on-screen instructions, and you will have Ventura up and running in no time. And if you are unsure, this guide or any Apple Store will have resources and experts to assist.

What Is iCloud and How Do I Use It?

- iCloud is a cloud storage service. Head to System Preferences > Apple ID > iCloud to choose what data you would like to synchronize and store.

How can I customize my Mac on Ventura for easier use?

macOS Ventura offers a plethora of accessibility features, from larger text to voice control. Head to System Settings -> Accessibility to tailor your Mac experience to your needs.

How Can I Set Up and Use Email?

- Launch the "Mail" app and follow the guided setup. Input your email and password, and the Mail app will take care of the rest.

I am worried about potential issues. How can I revert to my previous macOS if needed?

Always back up your data before any upgrade. With a backup, you can revert to a previous macOS version using Time Machine. While Ventura is designed to be stable and efficient, it is always good to have a safety net.

19 CONCLUSION & BONUS

The dawn of macOS Ventura is more than an OS upgrade; it is a call to rediscover the digital realm. And as seniors, this renaissance is not about catching up, but rather enriching our wisdom with newfound skills. Just as we once transitioned from letters to emails, we have now dived deeper into the cyber universe, armed with the power of Ventura. The essence of Ventura, like all Apple creations, lies in its simplicity and user-friendliness. Each feature is a bridge, not a barrier. Tech, like time, waits for no one. It evolves, shifts, and transforms. But so do we. As you have navigated macOS Ventura, you have not only adapted but thrived. This is not the end but the beginning of a more engaged, enlightened digital journey. Venture with Ventura, for every day is a new digital story waiting to be told.

Scan the QR code below to be directed to a web page where you can access 4 incredible bonuses. After providing your email address, you will receive 3 online video lessons and a list of tips and tricks about the use of macOS Ventura. Your participation and feedback are greatly appreciated!

LINK: https://topnotchinternational.aweb.page/macosventura-firstbonuspage

Made in the USA
Las Vegas, NV
05 July 2024

91860915R10057